IT TAKES TWO
OUR STORY

IT TAKES TWO

our story

JONATHAN *and* DREW SCOTT

HOUGHTON MIFFLIN HARCOURT
BOSTON / NEW YORK / 2017

CONTENTS

ACKNOWLEDGMENTS

Actually, it takes more than two when it comes to capturing a lifetime in 75,000 words, give or take. When we decided to write a memoir, we thought it would be an easy flip—no structural damage, toxic exposure, or hidden problems to deal with. Wow, were we wrong. It turned out to be a journey through memories we hadn't thought about in a very long time. More highs and lows than we could have imagined, and a fresh reminder of the incredible people whose support made our biggest reveal possible. It's humbling to think back and realize how many forks we've had in the road and how many folks have helped us choose the right path.

We were blessed from the beginning to be surrounded by wonderful role models who helped teach us about the importance of kindness, respect, compassion, and perseverance. From our incredible teachers at church and school, to our karate sensei, Gary Johnson, who was tough on us but understood that one day the discipline we'd learn would be invaluable. Our basketball coach, Mike Shannon, always knew exactly what to say to bring out the best in us . . . even when we felt like there was nothing left. Shelly Evans, our drama teacher, encouraged us to find our own voices and express our passions by digging deep within to get to the core of who we were. Many of these influences in our lives, who began in positions of authority to us, later became friends and remain a valuable part of our lives today. Nina Fowell comes directly to mind, and she has seen us through almost three decades of our development. No matter where we go or what we do, she takes the time to reach out and ask how WE are and if WE are finding happiness. What started out as a couple of rambunctious twins in her sixth grade class has evolved into a lifelong friendship.

When it comes to our peers, our pals, our partners in crime, completely different criteria establish the impact they've had on our lives. Let's be honest . . . we'd get up to no good from time to time. Nothing criminal or destructive, but definitely some good old-fashioned mischief. Our closest friends have always been genuine, reliable, trustworthy people. You'll find a lot of similarities in Pedro, Brad, Toni, Jodi, Mike, Simpson, Barb, and the rest of our eclectic mix of compadres. Not only were we comfortable exposing our most embarrassing moments to each other . . . but we discovered the importance of laughing hard every day. We've traveled together, lived together, and seen each other through personal triumphs and tragedies. There has never been a situation where we needed one of these guys, and they didn't drop everything to get to us. That's true friendship.

Our world changed when a company called Cineflix approached us to do what we now know as *Property Brothers*. There were many hands over the years involved in making it come together, such as Glen Salzman, Katie Ruttan Daigle, Christle Leonard, Gerard Barry, Lindsey Weidhorn, and Jessica Vander Kooij, but in the end we owe a huge debt of gratitude to the whole talented team of TV wizards. We have become like family with our crews for all our shows, and some days we're amazed we get any work done because you make us laugh so much. Particularly you, Marnie. After completing the pilot episode, we met our first incredible network partner, Corus, in Canada, where Vibika Bianchi, John MacDonald, Doug Murphy and their team took a big risk on some hosts that were doing things a little differently and a concept that might or might not pay off. Fortunately for all of us, it did. Soon after, the show was picked up in the U.S. by Scripps Networks, and we found remarkable allies in Kathleen Finch, Audrey Adlam, Allison Page, Shannon Driver, Lynne Davis, Loren Ruch, Victoria Chiaro, Abbi McCollum, Santos Lopez, and many more who would once again prove that good, passionate, talented people create even better things together. The relationships have always been ones of mutual respect, open communication, and joint effort. It has paid off in creating something magical that our audiences absolutely love. And speaking of audiences . . . we legitimately have the most amazing fans in the world. We love every opportunity we get to meet them face to face to show our gratitude. Your support is what fuels us through the long hours and grueling schedule.

When our world evolved and our television careers took off, we really needed to grow our team to ensure we could keep up. We have a few simple rules: First, we work with passionate people who love what they're doing and are genuinely great at it. Second, we only work with people that we like to work with. Sounds simple, but in reality it's harder to find than you would expect. Matt Horowitz was one of our first hires, when we were still mostly unknown. He has all of the good attributes of an amazing agent, but also a soul. His guidance, advice, and friendship have been invaluable and have definitely helped steer our ever-growing ship in the right direction. He heads our hard-working team at CAA, including Carla Laur, Cait Hoyt,

Stephanie Paciullo, Kate Childs, and a ton of other brilliant people who work tirelessly with our legal guru David Dembroski to keep us in line. We pride ourselves in being easy to work with . . . though our business is QUITE complex.

There are so many people we've worked with in the past who really did help make us a household name. There was our first publicist, Alina Goldstein Duviner, who we'll never forget meeting during the launch of the first season of *Property Brothers*. She looked us right in the eye and said, "We're going to make this show a hit." She was right. There was also The Door in NYC, who propelled us to the next level and personified what it meant to have a think tank of creative masterminds.

Inevitably over time, we grew our internal team to reflect the precision and efficiencies we've always strived to achieve in all our businesses. Lance, Josie, Richard, Christina, Stephanie, Rachel, Ashley, Amara, Ydo, Vanessa, and the rest of Team Scott are simply rock stars. We've always wanted to run a company that people love to work for and boasts an environment that keeps the team members challenged but excited to come in every day. We pulled it off, and are so proud of the squad we've assembled. They enable us to take on far more than we could ever do on our own while still keeping the bar raised higher than anybody else in the business. It allows us to pursue passion projects like this book which, thanks to our hero and editor, Justin Schwartz, and the HMH team—Marina Padakis Lowry, Tai Blanche, Rita Sowins, and Eugenie S. Delaney—we're sure will be another big success. Tamara, we'll admit the way you cracked the whip to get the good stuff out of us is simply superb.

If you've noticed . . . we don't do anything half-assed. We also don't pursue business relationships for the short term. We want relationships that are going to last and people we want to keep around for a very long time. It's the only way to build a legacy brand. But if you were to strip back all of the business and all of the shows and focus on the people who have personally had the most impact on us, it's family and the loves of our lives. Our parents, Jim and Joanne, you absolutely astonish us with your infinite love and support. You brought us into this world, but you also made us shine. Our brother JD, you have always been an ear if we needed to talk, muscle if we needed help, and right there when we needed anything. Thank you for putting up with a couple of annoying little clones your whole life. We've always looked up to you, big brother. We also can't forget Gracie and Stewie, because even though they're fur-babies . . . they're part of the family, and even while writing this sentence, they're staring up at us with unwavering love and devotion. Or maybe they just want to be fed. LOL.

And lastly, our beautiful soulmates, Linda and Jacinta, you make everything an adventure and breathe life into our souls. As much as we try to express it, you'll never fully understand the extent to which we appreciate you. Twins have a very special bond and nothing can break that. But we both agree that of all the people on this big, blue planet, you are the only two we want to share that with. We love you. We cherish you. And we look forward to every little reveal the future holds for us.

—Drew & Jonathan

IT HAS BEEN SAID THAT <u>FAMILY</u> AND <u>LOVE</u> ARE
THE TWO MOST IMPORTANT THINGS IN LIFE.
WE HAVE BEEN BLESSED WITH BOTH.

-Mom & Dad

FOREWORD

"Doctor, I think there's another baby."

We had just welcomed our son Jonathan into the world at 9:57 a.m. that spring morning at St. Paul's Hospital in Vancouver, British Columbia. But now the nurse had just delivered the surprise of our lives—at 10:01 a.m., Drew magically appeared. Within the span of four minutes on April 28, 1978, our family of three had become five.

The new duo launched their act on an unsuspecting world with no instruction book provided. Looking into their precious faces, we wondered what life had in store for them. Little did we know what they had in store for us!

Our firstborn son, James Daniel (JD), was still a month shy of his second birthday when his twin brothers arrived. With three children in diapers, Dad decided it was time to leave his job in the motion-picture industry for a career that would keep him closer to home. He became a child and youth counselor in Maple Ridge, about 30 miles east of Vancouver, where we lived and raised horses. That job afforded the flexibility we needed on the home front once Joanne returned to her work for a law office.

As time went by, Drew and Jonathan followed the unofficial twin rule book, bonding close and chattering in a secret language that only big brother JD could translate. Fortunately we were eventually all communicating on the same page.

Raising three rambunctious boys brought numerous daily challenges. That missing instruction book would have been helpful, but we learned a lot from those experiences and honed our problem solving skills in short order.

All three boys became excellent horseback riders. We did a lot of camping in those early days, often with the horses; the boys loved it. We would hike, ride, fish for trout, and sing around the campfire. Drew and Jonathan were constantly making up their own songs and certainly kept us all entertained.

By the time they were 8, the writing was already on the wall: They had launched their first business—selling decorative hangers—and went global. They had also started learning Shotokan karate, which sparked their competitive streak but also instilled the self-discipline, confidence, and sense of honor that defines them to this day.

But their real passion was in performing. Jonathan taught himself magic and earned national recognition while still in his teens, while Drew shined in theater and on the basketball court. As they entered adulthood, we prayed we had given them the necessary tools (no pun intended) to have a happy and successful life—without becoming starving artists.

They bought and flipped their first house at just 18, and the $50,000 profit they made became the seed money for what has become, twenty years later, as much a thriving dream factory as a business. It hasn't been all sunshine and roses, though.

Life happens, and parents are only as happy as their saddest child. Jonathan suffered anguish and heartache through a divorce, and Drew faced many a closed door in his early years pursuing his dream of an acting career. Notwithstanding this, they have always had a strong determination and have been relentless in their ability to forge on. The right doors did eventually open.

A huge part of their year is taken up with filming their five shows, book signings, Scott Living engagements, host appearances, commercial shoots, and social media. Jonathan and Drew often bring fans behind the scenes of their shows.

We love watching "the Scott brothers" have so much fun interacting with the fans—and the fans, in turn, enjoy asking us all kinds of questions about what the guys were like growing up. The most common one is whether they always got along so well. That answer is easy: Drew and Jonathan were best friends from the beginning and had a knack for working out differences so they could quickly get back to more important agendas of work or play. Their secret language of twins became unspoken.

This book serves as a portal into the ever-surprising, inspiring, and entertaining lives of two of our three wonderful sons. It showcases their joyful moments, painful struggles, relentless determination, and boundless optimism, all of which helped shape the fine men they are today. Their integrity, strong values, and love for their family make us so proud to be their parents.

We are a very close family, which is a gift that has paid itself forward throughout our lives. We talk every day, no matter how many miles separate us, and we often get calls from Jonathan or Drew inviting us to hop on a plane to join them in some adventure or come visit them on set. (The latter call occasionally comes with the announcement that sends shivers through us: "We have homework for you.")

In writing this engaging book, Jonathan and Drew are welcoming you into their world, both private and public. We sincerely hope you enjoy the journey—and the surprises they continue to bring—as much as we have.

Sincerely,

James and Joanne Scott

(Mom & Dad)

P.S. To their many fans all over the world, we thank you from the bottom of our hearts for embracing our family with love and kindness. You have given our sons their success, and we will never forget it. Our wish for each and every one of you is that you, too, will find fulfillment and happiness in your lives.

YOU INSPIRE US EVERY DAY
AND ARE THE REASON WE LOVE WHAT WE DO.
YOU LET US INTO YOUR HOMES AND YOUR HEARTS.
YOU ARE AMAZING.
YOU ARE LIKE FAMILY.
YOU ARE THE BEST FANS IN THE WORLD.
THIS BOOK WE DEDICATE TO YOU.

WE DIDN'T GROW
UP WITH FANCY
TOYS OR EXPENSIVE
THINGS TO PLAY
WITH. WE GREW UP
WITH EACH OTHER.
—Drew

Jonathan

Drew

Jonathan *Drew*

Drew *JD* *Jonathan*

Comments by Jonathan

GET A JOB

Birthdays were always fun for us growing up—our parents didn't need to get a bouncy castle or hire some event planner to make them special. There would always be ice cream cake and presents, maybe a clown and a round of Happy Meals with our friends at McDonald's, and once, even a trip to a water park. But the best birthdays were the ones when the family just saddled up our horses and rode to the national park at the edge of our farm in Maple Ridge, British Columbia. We'd cook some steaks for dinner, then sing around the campfire while Dad strummed his guitar. No rented bouncy castle could ever match that.

Jonathan was

(Besides, when it came to bouncing, Jonathan and I would rather pile up sofa cushions and mattresses and leap off the back deck, anyway.)

So when we woke up one April morning on what we assumed would be just another typical birthday, we had no idea our lives were about to change—until Dad made a surprise announcement: It was time for The Talk.

Jonathan and I exchanged eager looks, but tried to act cool (correction: I acted cool, and Jonathan tried to) as the three of us sat down at the kitchen table. We were growing up, and our parents had obviously taken note. That day, it turned out, we had reached an important milestone. Dad looked us each in the eye, man to man, then spelled it out for us in his thick brogue:

"Boys, you're seven years old," he decreed. "It's time to get a job."

We didn't stop to ask whether our Lego habit had forced Dad to borrow from the mob, or if the extra money was needed to send Jonathan to a sleep lab so he'd stop trying to walk through our bedroom wall in the middle of the night like some possessed zombie on an invisible treadmill. (Hilarious unless you happen to have the exact same DNA and have to spend every night of your life worrying that the same freak gene will eventually turn you into a wall-zombie, too.)

When we got older, we would understand and appreciate what Dad was instilling in us that day. He wanted us to get experience off the farm, and learn the value of a dollar. But at 7, all we really cared about was the cash we were going to rake in. We were like those cartoon characters whose pupils turn into dollar signs while they count bags

What can I say? I'm an active sleeper. I don't have to be conscious to go places!

Dad

Mom

Drew

Jonathan

Jonathan

Drew

BIG HAIR, HIGH
SHORTS, AND FUNKY
HATS ARE KINDA
OUR THING.
-Drew

Ha! Sounds like maybe you're jealous you were never asked to help.

of money in their heads. This wasn't like having to do chores for an allowance: This was grown-up, and we were excited to join the labor force. We grabbed the newspaper to start combing through the Help Wanted ads, crossing jobs off as we went.

ACCOUNTANT—Nice salary! I just so happened to love math and had some impressive skills when it came to figuring out how many apples Jane had left after Bobby ate three, but we were only in second grade and hadn't made it through the multiplication tables yet, so that could be an issue on the way up the corporate ladder. I marked that one MAYBE.

REPAIRMAN —There wasn't a small appliance in the house that Jonathan couldn't fix, but on the down side, he didn't discriminate between things that were actually broken and things that were perfectly fine before he started tearing stuff apart. And he tended to get distracted and wandered off mid-task. For days. Sometimes weeks. That one got a big, fat NO.

The Help Wanted ads weren't being very helpful. The whole thing seemed rigged toward people who knew how to drive, had previous experience, or—I strongly suspected—could even do long division.

"Do we have experience?" I wondered aloud.

"Rocks," Jonathan pointed out.

That was true. No one could boast anywhere near the experience we had in rock-picking. Ever the thrifty Scotsman, our dad used to send us out to clear the pastures by hand, paying us a nickel for each pail we filled with rocks. We could make enough to buy a box of our favorite

You mean too cheap to buy a power rake.

shortbread cookies or some cheap toy on a good day, but it was boring work and took forever, which is probably why the entire national labor force of rock-pickers consisted of prison road gangs and a pair of squirrely twins from Maple Ridge. We had a complicated love/hate relationship with rock-picking, and were secretly relieved that no one was advertising for professionals in that field.

The rest of our resume consisted of collecting bottles and cans for recycling, and rounding up abandoned shopping carts in the grocery store parking lot so we could return them to their racks to collect the quarter deposit. A friend with a paper route had also let us fill in for him when he went on vacation once, but, like Dad's rocks, the payoff just didn't seem to justify the time and labor involved. We wanted to get richer quicker. And have fun while we were at it. Karate, for example, was fun. A karate job would be just the ticket. We took lessons at a local dojo and were getting good at it, but we weren't ninja bodyguard material yet. And Maple Ridge wasn't the kind of place where people needed to hire a ninja yellow-belt bodyguard, anyway, much less a matching set. Still, we would definitely keep our eyes peeled for future opportunities there.

"We could sell something instead," I suggested. If no one would hire us, we'd just become our own bosses. We could always build a lemonade stand. Who didn't like lemonade?! Unfortunately, it wasn't the lemonade part of that rhetorical question that was the deal-breaker—it was the "who" part. We lived on the edge of the city, where residential homes were mixed in with rural farms, so unless it turned out that cows had pockets, a disposable income, and an unquenchable thirst for something besides slobbery trough water, no way were we going to be able to drum up enough customers for a steady lemonade

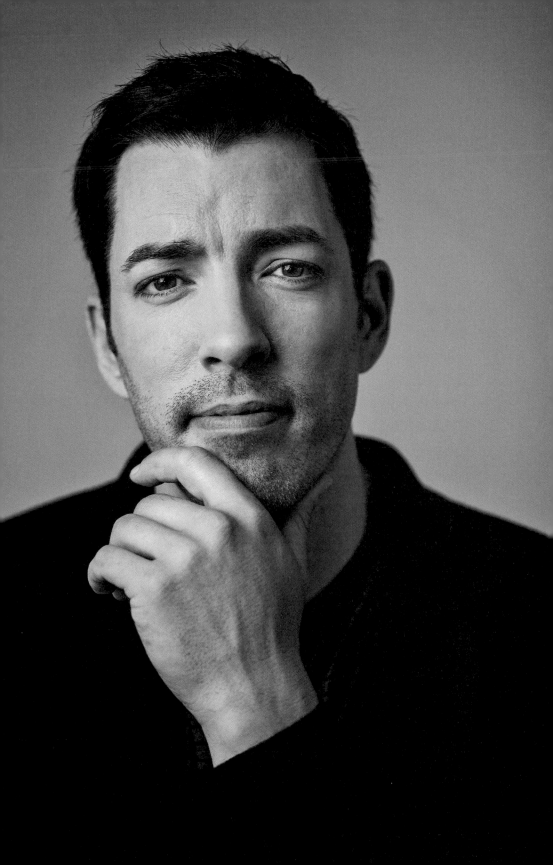

income. Or even much of a sporadic one, for that matter. Still, the idea of making something to sell was what intrigued us the most, so we kept brainstorming.

One weekend, we were poking through a crafts fair with our mom when we spotted some decorative hangers for sale. Wire hangers were the coat closet equivalent of rocks in the horse pasture—on their own, they were worthless and had a way of always mysteriously multiply-ing when you weren't looking. But here they were at the crafts fair, wrapped in colorful nylon ribbon, with people paying nearly $2.00 each for them! Jonathan and I picked one up for a closer look and quickly figured out how the simple knots were tied; it was sort of like the square-braiding every Cub Scout learns in order to make a lanyard keychain no parent in the history of the universe actually ever used. We could definitely DIY these hangers. Mom agreed to help with the tricky little rosettes at the top of each hanger, and JAM Enterprises was officially launched. (The company name stood for Jon, Andrew and Mom. None of us goes by the names our parents have always called us—I shortened mine, Jonathan lengthened his, and our older brother ditched his altogether to go by JD instead of James Daniel.)

The wire hangers themselves were free, and the material to wrap them was just five bucks for a big roll, so our overhead was low and our profits were steep—we were able to charge $1.75 for each hanger, which cost us all of fifty cents to make. We got good enough at wrap-ping them that we could knock out a hanger in ten (me) to twenty (Jonathan) minutes. But we weren't working for ice cream cones any-more: We had our eyes on a much bigger prize.

When we were 5 years old, we had gotten to visit Dad's native Scotland for the first time on a family vacation. Seeing all the medieval

plaid

cliff-top castles and learning the colorful history of brave clansmen and noble knights got us hooked on our heritage long before Mel Gibson made kilts cool again. We wanted to wave our family flag and wear the Scott coat of arms. We wanted to learn how to play bagpipes. But what we wanted most of all was a real sword. And by real, I mean a six-foot-long, two-edged claymore like the ones used by the original Highlanders.

It cost around $1,200.

Sure, it was a big number, but when you're in second grade, $10 and $10,000 might as well be the same, because they both appear in your undeveloped little brain in the file marked "a lot." They say that knowledge is power, but sometimes ignorance is a better running mate. You can't be overwhelmed when you're still too young to even be whelmed yet. We just dug in and started working like crazy. Our parents gave us a list of family and friends we could try selling our hangers to and gave us permission to sell door-to-door as well. We worked up a sales pitch and tag-teamed everyone with the charm offensive. The trick was to keep the patter going back and forth between the two of us so no one had the chance to interrupt and say no.

"You can bring some color to your closets," I would suggest.

"And the soft fabric we wrap them in means no more hanger indents on your clothes," Jonathan pointed out.

"You'll know whose hangers are whose in your house by the color-coding," I added. There was even a discount for bulk orders, in case your family was large and being torn apart by constant conflict over hanger ownership.

We used our top selling point to really clinch the deal: Each and every hanger was carefully crafted by hand to ensure the best quality.

Is that even a word?
Maybe you should stick to math.

We were determined to have a respectable sword fund by the time the family returned to Scotland in five years, with maybe a few bucks left over to buy some Oor Wullie comic books. Oor Wullie was a spiky-haired kid who was always cooking up crazy get-rich-quick schemes that generally ended with the town constable giving chase and Wullie complaining, "I nivver get ony fun roond here!" We could relate to that. We had no time for fun anymore, either. We told our friends we couldn't play because we had hangers to crochet. It made us go a little Martha Stewart. We started fiddling with different color combinations (blue-and-white was a hit; brown-and-yellow, not so much) and even scouted displays in the home section at K-Mart and local department stores to get an idea of what color schemes people liked best. We rolled out special holiday editions—red-and-green hangers for Christmas, orange-and-black for Halloween—because who wouldn't want to decorate their home for the holidays with coat hangers?

Then we scored the kind of jackpot small business owners dream about: We knocked on the door of a woman who turned out to own a chain of Americana gift shops in Japan. JAM Enterprises was going global, baby! We would probably be able to buy two swords and a battle-ax at this rate!

Hanger demand had always outpaced supply, but now it was out of control, even with the freelance help of our brother, JD. To make matters worse, we were hamstrung by the labor restrictions of a factory fore-mom who forced us to shut down during school hours and at bathtime every night. We realized it was time to expand. We were going to have to subcontract. Our classmates were excited to earn their own money, too, so we set up workshop in our living room and paid

JON ANDREW MOM ENTERPRISES
"WE TAKE CARE OF YOUR HANG-UPS"
467-0667

Jonathan   *Drew*

WORK HARD,
PLAY HARDER
-Drew

Umm, you only get grounded if you get caught. And I'm too good for that.

everyone twenty-five cents per hanger, assigning them just the long, straight bottom stretches of wire—Jonathan and I did the tricky corners ourselves for quality control. We watched Care Bear marathons on TV while we worked. With each finished hanger, I tracked our profits on my mental abacus like a gambler counting cards. The next time we went to the Highlands, I calculated, we could get swords, shields, and armor to start a serious gladiator collection.

We didn't pay Mom for her rosettes.

Predictably, both the hanger market and our interest in sitting inside all day to make them fizzled out after a year or so, but we weren't ready to take early retirement and spend the rest of our days playing miniature golf and sipping virgin piña coladas poolside. We were obsessed with watching the balance grow in our bank passbooks. Back to the newspaper's classified section we went to see what opportunities might be awaiting us now that we had run our own business. Maturity, experience, and managerial skills were on our side now, even if we couldn't drive or work during school hours. Or evenings. Or holidays. Or whenever Jonathan got grounded for being a brat.

This time, our eyes fell on an ad the Parks and Recreation Department had placed. They wanted to hire clowns for birthday parties and parades. All you needed to do was sign up for six Saturdays of clown class and pass your clown finals to earn official clown certification.

This was a no-brainer. We were born performers! We were always putting on shows for our parents and friends. I had acting in my blood and Jonathan was funny without even trying. We showed up for the Parks and Rec class and took our seats alongside the grown-up wan-

Now that, I can definitely agree with. And Drew is a total drama queen.

nabe clowns, who all cast dismissive *"awww, aren't they cute"* looks our way. Clowns are kind of cutthroat, come to find out.

We loved clown school and aced every test of clown competency, from twisting balloons into dachshunds to juggling tennis balls (or oranges, or stuffed animals, or pretty much three of anything except rocks, which we still resented.)

We also learned some beginner's magic tricks and how to apply clown make-up. I wore a bald cap with a tiny hat on it and became Curly the Clown, while Jonathan put on a rainbow wig and called himself Dimples. We graduated magna cum laude at the top of our clown class and were immediately hired by Parks and Rec to start working parades, festivals, and birthday parties for ten bucks a pop. We couldn't believe we were getting paid to goof off. Our sword fund kept steadily growing.

The novelty of becoming a different person with traits I could pick and choose is probably what first gave me the acting bug as a kid. I liked to experiment with different characters, which is great if you're trying out a new pratfall at a kid's birthday party, but not so great if you think you're on *Inside the Actors Studio* and start overanalyzing your "craft" as Curly the Clown. Which is how I came to think I could wow the audience with my Pacino-like range by playing a sad clown once in a local parade. I moped my way along the parade route, head hung low, swiping at invisible tears and occasionally pulling an oversized tissue from my clown sleeve to blow my round clown nose melodramatically. The puzzled looks and lack of appreciative murmurs from the curb-side spectators made me realize soon enough that no one wanted to watch a depressed clown turn a holiday parade into the Bataan Death March, but by then I was committed to the character and had to see it through. One thing our parents taught us from the time we were small was to always finish what you started. It was part of a so-called "cowboy code" that our dad drilled into all three of us boys when we were growing up.

There are lots of interprctations of the unwritten Old West code of honor out there, attributed to everyone from Zane Grey to the Texas Rangers, but the version that served as our family's moral Mapquest boiled down to a set of principles as simple and straightforward as they were timeless, among them:

1. Take pride in every task, no matter how big or small
2. Finish whatever you start
3. Never break a promise
4. Don't turn your back on someone in need
5. Ride for your brand

Our work ethic, plus the hyper energy and slapstick humor that we came with, soon turned us into the reigning junior Bozos of Maple Ridge. (Not everyone was cheering us on: One adult rival seemed to think we were somehow cheating by being twins, and would loudly groan, "Not *those* two again" if we were hired for the same gig.)

Moms started asking for us specifically when they booked a party through Parks and Rec, and after a while, we realized that we had enough of a fan base to branch out on our own and rake in a whole lot more than ten or twenty an hour. The going rate in the private sector was $50 to $100 per hour. We made business cards and flyers and became rogue clowns. Rogue clowns in high demand. We even kicked it up a notch by investing in drywaller stilts so we could add a character named Stretch to our repertoire. Stretch came perilously close to becoming Squash early on when Jonathan decided to suit up and march out to the pasture where our horse Ringo was grazing to see if he could swing his stilt-leg over Ringo's bare back. Ringo, it is important to note, was not your typical stallion, and only really liked children. He'd let you do just about anything, but if *any* of our horses wanted to be straddled by an 8-foot, polka-dotted clown, it was not going to be Ringo. Mom spotted Jonathan in the nick of time and ran out back to tell him to step AWAY from the horse.

By the time we boarded the plane for a return trip to Scotland the summer we were 10, we had saved several thousand dollars—enough to afford not only swords and some shortbread, but probably our own knights and a round table as well. Maybe not a round table. Maybe a rectangular, 7-foot one with a live edge, custom-made from a slab of reclaimed acacia. Whatever, we would be totally prepared in the event medieval Vikings ever showed up to pillage Greater Vancouver.

We had no intention of blowing our whole nest egg at once, though—we were too hooked on the challenge of seeing how much we could make and save, and a zero balance in our passbook would have seriously bummed us out. Our sense of pride shot to the moon once we arrived in Scotland: Our parents forgot to alert the bank they were traveling abroad, and their credit cards were temporarily frozen. It was up to us to save the family vacation. We happily floated Dad a loan.

We left Scotland that summer with Oor Wullie comic books, a case of Scotland's favorite Irn-Bru soda, plus our coveted claymore, and two broadswords, starting a collection that would become a lifelong obsession. (Yes, we have worn the custom-made suit of armor displayed in the great room of our Las Vegas house, and yes, it looks best on me.)

Even better, we left with the simple, unshakeable conviction that

Careful, your head won't fit in that helmet . . .

15

would carry us from decorating hangers to running a multi-million dollar empire with over 200 full-time and contract employees today: Nothing is out of reach if you're willing to work hard. That challenge our dad threw down on our 7th birthday was the most useful multiplication table I ended up learning: Dream x effort = reward. No matter how big or small your dream is, if your effort is zero, you're going to end up with zero at the end of the day. Likewise, the greater your effort, the bigger your reward.

People say good things come to those who wait. I like to say that's because the great things are already taken. You have to work really hard to get yourself ready for opportunities as they come. That takes preparation, education, and determination. Luck has nothing to do with it.

We stuck with our clowning business until we hit high school and started itching for a new venture. We both still thrived on entertaining people, but applying and taking off our clown makeup felt like the world's biggest time-suck once we were teenagers. Plus, Jonathan was deep in the throes of a clown identity crisis: Dimples sounded too babyish now that he was in eighth grade, and he had to establish street cred because image was everything in the eyes of high school girls. When a well-respected clown about town named Bubblegum retired, Jonathan snapped up the name and created a new character. Because if you're Jonathan, and you've fallen out of the top bunk as many times as he did before Mom finally said enough and gave us our own rooms, your thought process, too, would go something like this: *Nobody will ever take me seriously as Dimples, but the name Bubblegum? That's legit!*

High school changed the equation for us in another way as well: We became a trio instead of a duo, thanks to a kid named Pedro. Pedro, who is actually Iranian and named Pedram, caught our attention when

Let the hair obsession begin!

Drew

Jonathan

WHEN YOU SHARE A ROOM, BUNK BEDS,
AND A FACE WITH SOMEBODY,
YOU BECOME INSEPARABLE!
-Drew

we were out knocking around tennis balls on a public court one after-noon and Pedro kept riding past slowly on his bicycle, dinging a little bell. "Do we know that guy?" I wondered, after about the thirty-eighth time Pedro had dinged us. "Isn't he that new kid in our homeroom? Maybe he wants to play us," Jonathan said. That would be fun—we could totally destroy him on the court. *Ding-ding, ding-ding.* "Hey, c'mere!" we called over.

Pedro did, in fact, want to play us, and after accepting our mag-nanimous offer to join the game, he proceeded to whip our butts. He was equally good when it came to volleying one-liners and insults, too. The three of us became instant best friends for life. Pedro was like a long-lost brother, the Persian triplet separated from us at birth. Mom and Dad considered him a member of our family, and Pedro's very traditional parents in turn counted us as part of their huge, extended clan (we were *deraaz-ali,* "tall, skinny white kids.")

Pedro was eager for us to impress the relatives, including some who would fly in from Iran for feasts and celebrations. Pedro taught us how to count to ten in Farsi, and had us stand up at the table, in front of five generations of their family, to proudly recite our numbers. Everyone's jaws dropped. Then Pedro's mother reached over to playfully slap me. Pedro, we discovered, had taught us some of the worst swear words in the Persian language. Fortunately, our unintentional gutter-mouths didn't keep the party from ending the way they always did at Pedro's, with the guests all singing and dancing. That warm family vibe and their joy at just being together definitely helped inspire us years later when we set about designing and building our Las Vegas dream home: What we wanted more than anything was a place where everyone we loved could come together to relax, have fun, and just hang out with each other. Singing and dancing optional but encouraged, Pictionary and Ping-Pong mandatory.

At school, skateboarders were the self-anointed alpha kids. We didn't skateboard; cool as that was, it wasn't our jam. Besides, we weren't the type of kids to pour everything into a single pursuit. That would be like deciding to eat Brussels sprouts and nothing else. Never gonna happen. Jonathan, Pedro, and I were all over the map in terms of all of our interests and skills—we were athletes, but also nerds; we were driven and goal-oriented, but we devoted as much effort to our pranks as we did to our studies and money-making schemes. I felt like I was in my zone whether I was playing on the basketball team or rehearsing with the drama club. If we were interested in some activity, we just went for it, without stopping to worry whether we "belonged" to any particular group.

We had at least a toe in most of the usual high school cliques, and that fluidity turned us into our own clique: We were confident but never stuck up (cowboy code), and we pretty much ran the school like ambassadors-at-large. The clown suits may have been mothballed, but entertaining people and cracking them up was still our life's mission, and we were smooth talkers who could get away with a lot. We would've been grounded until we were 27 if our parents knew half the stuff we did. Pedro was a willing and worthy accomplice.

Our first big business venture with Pedro on board came in ninth grade, when we spotted these little personal safety devices called Kimo Blasters at a home show. They were marketed to attach to a purse or belt so you could pull a cord to emit an ear-splitting alarm if threatened. Sort of like bear spray for muggers and creepers.

Jonathan and I had discovered our knack for sales in elementary

unsuspecting instigator

19

school, when we decided we wanted to do something exciting for our class. We created a competition around our favorite book series. The best-selling mystery novels by Eric Wilson were the Canadian equivalent of the Hardy Boys, and we were eager to turn our friends on to the adventures of Tom and Liz Austen in such classics as *Terror in Winnipeg* or *Vampires of Ottawa*. As head of the Eric Wilson Fan Club at school, I had a vested interest in ginning up membership.

We bought (or maybe snuck into a field and dug up?) a giant pumpkin, brought it to school, and announced that it would be the grand prize in our contest, which, best as I can remember, involved answering questions about a mystery novel, or maybe drawing something from one of the plots. We hyped it every day, at every opportunity ("WHO WILL WIN THE GIANT PUMPKIN? YOU STILL HAVE A CHANCE!!"), stirring a sort of mob hysteria with our own over-the-top enthusiasm. It was like we were giving away the golden ticket to Willy Wonka's Chocolate Factory, except . . . not so much. We were giving away a mutant squash. Yet we were able to make everyone not only want a useless vegetable, but nearly riot over it. Once we'd discovered the power of persuasion, there was no going back. Which is why, in ninth grade, we decided to order fifty Kimo Blasters wholesale. Bought in bulk, they cost around four bucks each, but we figured we could sell them for at least twice that. Our sword fund had the capital to invest. And our hunch was right.

We sold out in a day.

Jonathan and Pedro started giddily crunching numbers and immediately wanted to bite off way more than I thought we could chew.

"What if we order 10,000 units?" Jonathan suggested. "Heck, if we had the money, we could get 100,000. Then we could make a million

JD

Drew

Jonathan

NOT EVERY IDEA WAS GROUNDBREAKING,
BUT THE LESSONS WE LEARNED
WERE INVALUABLE.
-Drew

Maybe he could load our bags.

dollars. If we *bought* a million, we could earn eight to ten million!" Pedro seconded the motion. I looked at the two of them with math-nerd pity, and shot them down with what I assumed was unassailable logic.

"Guys, no. The only reason we sold these was because of family and friends, and they're not buying any more. We've already saturated the natural market. Your projections are based on the market being warm, and the market is cold now."

Jonathan and Pedro were sure I was wrong and decided they'd just become blaster billionaires on their own, and maybe if I was lucky they would still invite me along for rides on their private jet.

They bought 300 more blasters, and sold maybe a couple of dozen door-to-door. They still stubbornly clung to the conviction that nationwide demand for personal alarms would skyrocket any day, and they would be the geniuses who had the market cornered. I'm all for positive thinking, but we're talking about a country so nonviolent that it's generally ranked just below Switzerland in lists of the world's safest places to live. There's a reason you haven't seen CSI: Nova Scotia. Jonathan and Pedro sat on those stupid boxes of unsold blasters for years, until Jonathan finally decided to unload them on a buyer who'd take them off his hands for pennies on the dollar. When he went to the boxes in storage to check the inventory, though, he discovered that our brother JD had gotten there first—he'd been quietly giving away the blasters as gag birthday and holiday gifts for years, and the boxes were empty.

Salesmanship wasn't a skill we only applied to the marketplace. We were lucky enough to attend a public school that was experimenting with an independent-learning model that let you complete courses

We should have gone into burglar alarms instead.

Parle pour toi.

at your own pace and allowed for a lot of creativity. Each course had twenty learning guides you had to complete for a year's credit. We were always trying to turn assignments into original performances to knock out learning guides faster. If we were supposed to master restaurant vocabulary in French class, we'd do some slapstick routine playing a bumbling waiter and a demanding customer at a Parisian café, and we'd end up with an A because the effort we put into entertaining everyone made up for our butchery of subjunctive verbs.

The school boasted state-of-the-art technology, including a professional editing suite, and we loved to spend countless hours writing, directing, filming, and acting in videos that we then convinced our teachers took at least as much time to produce as any book report.

Before we were born, our dad was in the film industry, starting out as a stunt rider on a bucking bronc for a beer commercial, then moving on to acting before working his way up to jobs behind the camera as the director of the second unit. He stayed in touch with a lot of friends from those days, even after he moved on to a career as a counselor who worked with troubled kids. Since socialization was part of the therapy, he often included one or both of us on their field trips. One time, when Warren, one of the kids, expressed a keen interest in movie-making, Dad arranged a visit to the set of *Look Who's Talking Too*, which was filming in Vancouver. I got to go along (wearing a white polyester suit) and met John Travolta and Kirstie Alley. Watching them bring a script to life, feeling the creative energy as the director and crew worked to make each scene flawless—even the routine, tedious parts of filmmaking grabbed my interest and excited me. *I want to do this*, I thought.

Our drama teacher, Mrs. Evans, had gone to high school with Michael J. Fox, and she used some connections she had with casting directors to send some of her students out on auditions. When we were 15 or 16, Jonathan and I started getting background work with our friend Toni and landed some small roles here and there. We even landed a spot in a national Molson Canadian air-miles commercial that aired during the Grey Cup, the Canadian equivalent of the Super Bowl. We played twins who look out an office building window and spot some guy marching in the street, then race down to join him, starting a sort of flash-mob parade.

Both of us knew by the time we graduated that we wanted a future in front of, and behind, the camera. We also knew that we didn't want to be starving artists. We needed a steady income to put this plan into motion.

Fresh out of high school, about to turn 18, we found ourselves right back where we had been at age 7: brainstorming ways to earn the money it would take to achieve our goal.

We didn't bother with the Help Wanted ads this time. We went straight for the cheesy infomercials on TV. Because who better to hang your entire future on than extremely loud strangers urging you to pulverize anything remotely edible (sunflower seeds, giant pumpkins) into delicious vitamin juice, or dial up a psychic to get an urgent message from the beyond ("Never wear plaid"). But wait, there's more! YOU CAN MAKE MILLIONS BY BUYING HOUSES WITH NO MONEY DOWN!!

That caught our interest. Operators didn't have to stand by long to wait for our order. We were no strangers to sweat equity: Besides learning how to fix things around the farm as we grew up, we had just finished helping Dad build a big house and barn on a ranch our parents had bought in Alberta, where we had enrolled at the University of

Calgary. The demand for student housing was always high; if we could just break into the real estate market, there was no way we wouldn't make a profit. Our first investment turned out not to be a purchase at all: It was a house with an old lease that students kept passing down to one another. The rent hadn't been raised in over a decade. A friend of a friend currently held it, and was leaving. We swooped in to take it over.

The place was a disaster. The basement was crammed with forty years of student crap. It looked like a fraternity house for hoarders. We hauled out seven truckloads of garbage, then finished the basement and created two additional bedrooms. That became our rent-free pad. We rented out all the rooms upstairs and cleared an $800-a-month profit. That became our seed money for the next project.

This time, we found a $200,000 eyesore near campus whose previous owner evidently had a stucco fetish and an incontinent cat. And possibly some sociopathic tendencies: Everything was painted blood red. The walls gave me angry dreams. Nobody thought we'd be able to do it, and it did take a mountain of paperwork, but we actually managed to get the murderous house for practically nothing: just $250 down.

That first house, in hindsight, was as easy as flipping would ever get. The fixes were mostly cosmetic—getting rid of the green shag carpet in the master bedroom, pulling stucco off the wall (accidentally taking big chunks of drywall with it), and repainting. We managed to turn five bedrooms into seven. All told, it took us three months. We lived rent-free in it for a year, renting out the extra bedrooms. Then we sold it and walked away with $50,000 clean profit.

Real estate, we decided, would be the perfect job to keep us afloat while we chased our real dreams.

BRO VS. BRO

Drew

The flip side of knowing your identical sibling so well is . . . knowing them so well. There was no learning curve when it came to pushing each other's buttons. We were both hardwired with the same owner's manual.

Naturally we squabbled like any brothers do—stupid stuff like, "stop breathing so loud"—but it rarely got physical. Unfortunately, our parents didn't specifically forbid psychological and biological warfare.

Our all-time Hall of Fame fight happened in ninth grade, when Jonathan and Pedro saved their lunches all week to stuff inside my locker, which they regularly broke into no matter how many times I changed the combination.

When I next opened my locker after a long weekend, a cloud of fruit flies emerged. As an added bonus, some rancid black slime was oozing all over my notebooks. I slammed the door shut and was already fuming when Jonathan and Pedro came up behind me in the hallway and snapped the strap on my backpack. The strap broke, and all my books went flying. I went flying, too—right after Jonathan and Pedro, who took one look at my face and ran for their lives. I caught Jonathan right in front of the school. I hoisted his entire body up like a wrestler with 'roid rage, then "*gently*" put him down onto the hood of an idling car waiting to pick some kid up in the Kiss and Ride lane. Jonathan wasn't hurt, but the mom behind the steering wheel kind of lost it.

Jonathan

Long before Drew hurled me into traffic in the Kiss and Die lane, Mr. I Never Touched Him left his mark. There's still a butt print on my head from him sitting on me in the womb.

Pedro and I may have played some mischievous, lighthearted pranks on him now and then, but we abided by all international peace treaties and inflicted no physical harm. As far as I know, there are no provisions in the Geneva Conventions covering fruit-fly combat. For the record, the way we got his locker combination was for one of us to stand on either side of him, and look over his shoulder. Again and again.

Because I am far too mature to whine about all the things Drew ever did to me, I've created a fun little game, instead, called

MATCH THE INJURIES (DREW) CAUSED TO JONATHAN WHILE TECHNICALLY NEVER LAYING A HAND ON HIM:

1. Scar over eyebrow

2. Stitches in lip

3. Wind knocked out of lungs

4. Dislocated pinky toe

5. Smashed nose

6. Giant goose egg to forehead

a. Badminton racket in doubles game

b. Elbow jab in basketball game

c. Karate move

d. Paintball

e. Extended hand interrupting running leap

f. Elbow jab in basketball game . . . again

WELL, WE'RE NOT GOING TO GIVE YOU THE ANSWERS HERE . . . HIT UP OUR FACEBOOK PAGES.

Jonathan

Drew

IT'S NOT THAT
WE DENY BEING
OVERACHIEVERS.
WE JUST PREFER
BEING CALLED
SUCCESSFUL
DREAMERS.
-Jonathan

Drew

Jonathan

JONATHAN

Comments by Drew

PURSUIT OF HAPPINESS

When we were kids growing up, Mom and Dad always dreamed of having their own ranch in the foothills of the Rocky Mountains.

Every summer, we'd load up the family station wagon with tents, sleeping bags, and the rest of our camping gear, then head through the deep valleys of British Columbia and over the mountains toward the big-sky prairies of Alberta, 600 miles along the Trans-Canada Highway. We passed the hours with our version of car karaoke, belting out the folk songs we'd sometimes perform as a family for the guests our parents led on trail rides back at our horse farm. If JD,

Drew, and I tried to mix it up with the pop songs we'd hear on the radio, Dad would put a stop to it. He didn't want Billie Jean knockin' at his door, and there was no way he was ever going to Walk Like an Egyptian or provide backup to Four Non-Blondes.

"It's not real music," he'd joke, "and the driver gets to pick the genre."

Rules are rules, so we'd usually wind up back at "Danny Boy" or "Scotland the Brave."

In the back seat, my brothers and I would play games, bicker, and try to make each other crack up until Dad's arm reached over to blindly swat at us. "Stop giggling like a bunch of schoolgirls!" he'd scold, which only made us laugh that much harder, and before we knew it, Dad was laughing too. If we grew too quiet, though, Dad would grow suspicious: Falling asleep on this road trip was strictly forbidden. "You'll waste the beautiful scenery!" he said, which left us silently pondering whether bighorn sheep were such attention-seekers that they would pack up and move to Florida if we didn't notice them for a 23rd or 24th—or 47th—time.

Dad is a rugged outdoorsman—the last person you'd ever find chanting "ohm" on a yoga mat—but he's always known how to be 100 percent present in a moment, whether roping cattle in the high country or just sitting on a fallen log, strumming his guitar. He'll tell you that he's as awestruck by the Canadian Rockies today as he was when he first laid eyes on them 64 years ago. He wanted us to know

So if ungrateful children didn't look, glaciers melt and the Rocky Mountains get sucked back into the earth.

By the way . . . the WORST seats in the wood-paneled station wagon were the rear-facing ones that put you on display for the car behind, but it was the only swat-free zone in the car . . .

that same sense of wonder, even though we'd gazed out the passenger windows at the same forests, crystal-blue lakes, and rugged mountain peaks every single summer of our lives on that drive. Nothing was to be taken for granted.

Still, I have to admit, Dad had a point we wouldn't fully realize or have perspective on until years later: It really is pretty spectacular scenery.

The trips to Alberta had been a tradition since we were babies. When we were toddlers Mom used to pin our sleeping bags tightly shut with giant diaper pins so we couldn't wriggle out in the middle of the night and freeze to death or wander off to become grizzly appetizers. When we got old enough to hold a tent pole reasonably straight, and could be trusted to drive the stakes into the ground instead of each other, we were expected to help pitch camp before going to explore the woods or catch some fish for dinner.

We'd take our time making our way through the Rockies, peeling off along the way for some great side adventures, like exploring the Gold Rush ghost town at a resort called Three Valley Gap, where we would stop to visit a famous old cowboy my parents knew. His name was Sky Floyd Drew, but everyone called him Sky Blue because he

Jonathan says "expected" because he and JD always bolted off and I was the only one who actually did help.

Ya snooze, ya lose!

dressed only in blue, from his cowboy hat down to his boots. Mom told us he once broke the world record for spinning the biggest vertical rope loop, tossing it from the top of the CN tower in Toronto.

Sky Blue hosted a Western revue every night at the Walter Moberly Theater at the resort, singing and performing fancy tricks with his lariat. When we were in the audience, he would throw his rope to lasso Drew or me, then bring us up on stage in front of hundreds of tourists from around the globe and make us part of the show. Neither of us was the least bit shy or reluctant. Having an audience excited us—even when it technically belonged to someone else. If ham-roping were in the Guinness Book, we probably could've clinched that record for Sky Blue, too. His performances got us all fired up about creating our own live shows someday, and maybe building our own Wild West town. Even back then, real estate and entertainment were twin ambitions, both literally and figuratively!

Drew and I had a lot of fun talking about our Western town, and even once built a cardboard-box version in Dad's office. But the idea didn't really take off until it was just Dad and me making the Alberta drive once when I was around 14, and I told him what Drew and I had been thinking.

A lot of parents probably would have just humored a kid with such a farfetched fantasy, or given him a reality check and shot it down right away. But Dad climbed right on board and started hashing out all the details with me. We spent much of the ten-hour drive talking about saloon brawls and stagecoach robberies and everything you'd have expected to see in a real mining town in the 1800s. Would we be able to track down or replicate antique fixtures to make the saloon feel authentic? Were gallows outside the jail an insurance liability, or just

Mom

Dad

JD

Drew

Jonathan

IF YOU EVER HAVE TROUBLE FINDING US . . .
IT'S BECAUSE WE ARE HAPPILY HIDDEN
IN THE MIDDLE OF NOWHERE.
-Jonathan

too big of a downer? Dad and I spent our whole trip discussing my imaginary town like a pair of deep-pocketed developers mapping out a model community. I called it Silver City, after a real silver mining town in the Banff area around the end of the 19th century. By the time we reached Alberta, Dad and I had worked out staffing, marketing, and even the types of stunts required to put on the ultimate show.

For our parents, though, Alberta beckoned as more than a vacation destination: It was their promised land.

Dad was born and raised in the medieval Scottish market town of Lanark, where rebel knight William Wallace first drew his sword in the name of independence for Scotland, slaying the English sheriff Haselrig in 1297. (Wallace was played by Mel Gibson some seven centuries later in *Braveheart*, the Hollywood version of the uprising.) Dad made his own big push for independence when he was 17, but it was a toilet plunger he wielded, not a sword, and the story never got made into a movie. It was pretty epic, though.

Dad was a horse lover who grew up watching Western movies and always pictured himself riding the open range someday with real-life cattlemen on a big ranch across the Atlantic. It wasn't just the cowboys' work that appealed to him: Dad also admired the simple, straightforward values of the frontier, where authenticity was more the measure of a man than ambition. He may have been entering adulthood at the dawn of the space race, but Dad was more captivated by rodeos than rocket ships.

At 17, he was working as a plumber's apprentice when a friend who knew the captain of the *Empress of Scotland* got him signed on to work as a lowly "fourth sanitary engineer" aboard the passenger ship. He would earn his passage to Montreal fixing toilets for the equivalent

Wow, even we made more picking rocks.

of 12 cents a day, but who was complaining? He was going to live out West at last!

When the *Empress* docked in Canada, Dad added his 96 cents in wages to the 20 dollars in life savings he had brought with him from Scotland. He took the first job offered, as a farmhand in Ontario.

The sour elderly couple that owned the farm worked Dad to the bone and fed him nothing but lettuce and tomatoes. He got up in time to milk the cows at 4 a.m. and finished the last of his chores around 9 p.m. The couple paid him 50 dollars a month, plus room and board. I never had the heart to ask him, but I'm assuming salad dressing was extra and there were no breadsticks.

During the fall harvest, when neighboring farmers pooled their labor, Dad learned from the other workers that the going wage for hired hands was actually 150 dollars a month—three times what he was earning. By then, the starvation diet, grueling hours, and sheer loneliness had worn Dad down. Canada was not what he had expected, and he was starting to seriously consider throwing in the towel and sailing back to Scotland. Instead, he took a winter job as a maintenance man for a hotel in Fort Erie, Ontario, where he soon befriended a guest who trained racehorses. Dad shared his frustration over not finding any jobs doing real cowboy work.

"Son, you're in the wrong place," the guest told him, "Alberta is where you need to be." That was where all the big working ranches were. "You'll do well there," he added.

The guest ended up buying Dad a bus ticket, pressing a few extra dollars into his hand, and putting him aboard a Greyhound bound for Calgary. Dad eagerly headed to the employment office as soon as he arrived.

"I want to be a cowboy," he announced.

Once they were done laughing, the clerks told him the ranchers did their hiring down at the bar of the Black Diamond Hotel.

Dad soon ended up exactly where he had always longed to be—on horseback all day long, roping cattle. Even better, he would later reminisce, the cattle were "wild as deer," demanding expert riding skills and tricky rope work to bring them down from the craggy mountain passes where they often roamed. Dad lived in a bunkhouse with the other cowboys, and was fed well enough to put on the weight he'd lost working for the miserly old couple.

Come summer, Dad decided to join a friend who was leading horseback trips through the backcountry in Banff. It was there, at a party one night, that Dad looked around the room and spotted a pretty girl with long blond hair. He walked up to her, fell to one knee, and asked her to marry him.

Mom was Toronto-born but had grown up riding horses and dreaming of coming out West to be a cowgirl. She and a girlfriend had banked enough money baby-sitting their way through high school to get to Banff after graduation. Mom was just 17. In Banff, she quickly learned how to ride Western and got hired by a guest ranch. She had no shortage of flirting cowboys and resort workers vying for her attention at the party that night when Dad appeared and blew the competition out of the water. She turned down his proposal-at-first-sight, but the bold move resulted in two years of dating (or courting, as Dad puts it) before the two of them eloped.

Someday, the newlyweds promised themselves, they would own their own horse ranch in Alberta, and build their dream home there. But work in Banff was seasonal, so they set out for Vancouver, where

Jonathan

the milder climate and bigger city offered better opportunities for a year-round income. When summer rolled around, they'd shift back to Banff for a couple of months to take advantage of the perfect weather in their slice of paradise. It was a pattern that continued well after having us kids, and it showed no sign of ending—even if we were begging and pleading for a little Disneyland action.

After Dad's riding skills landed him a bit role in a movie, he forged a new career as a stunt man. Mom was working her way up the ladder as a paralegal for a law firm in downtown Vancouver. Even after JD was born 10 years into their marriage, Mom would still pack up the baby to go spend time with Dad when he had to be away on location for weeks or even months at a time. Drew and I put an end to his celluloid cowboy days when we came along. Three babies on a movie set were too much to handle for even the mellowest parents.

We spent our childhood watching Mom and Dad pursue their lifelong dream and build the nest egg to make it reality, mostly from their savvy and sweat equity when it came to buying and selling the homes we lived in over the years. They'd always fix them up and make a nice profit. After they finally found the Alberta property they wanted, they turned their attention to the ranch house they wanted to build. And they did it themselves from the ground up, meticulously designing it down to the last doorknob.

When the time came to start construction, I agreed to change schools to spend the latter part of my tenth grade year in Alberta working alongside Dad on the place. My carpentry skills had expanded beyond the basics by then because I was constantly designing and building large illusions for my magic act. I could not only build the family a kitchen island, I could make it disappear, too.

*Now I feel bad I didn't
mail you some sarcastic rebuts.*

My move to Alberta was the first time I had ever left Drew's side for more than a few hours, though. We've always been best friends as well as brothers, and it felt weird not to have him right there 24/7, finishing my sentences or cracking the exact joke that had just crossed my mind, too.

It wasn't just Drew I missed—it was JD, our best friend, Pedro, and our whole crazy crew. Pulling pranks just doesn't deliver the same payoff if you have to play both perpetrator and victim. I've always been outgoing, though, and I figured I'd make new friends once I started school in High River, even if the pickings were a lot slimmer than I was used to. The town was barely a speck on the map—10,000 people, tops—and a lot sleepier than Maple Ridge. High River was about 30 miles and 50 light years south of Calgary, so my social life was about to get rural.

Still, I wasn't particularly stressed about being the new kid since I'd changed high schools once before, when Drew and I transferred to a new "work at your own pace" college-like public school where we both had thrived. I was a strong student and a good athlete, with a sense of humor that had always made me popular enough with both my classmates and the teachers, even if I was never one of the "popular kids." So what could possibly go wrong, right?

Not right.

To say my first day at Senator Riley High was a disaster would be like calling the Armageddon a mildly-warmer-than-average day with an elevated air-quality advisory. We're not just talking subtle buzz kill here: This was total, scorched-earth, take-no-prisoners buzz annihilation.

We were living in a motel for the time being, but Dad had to be out at the construction site and couldn't drop me at school that first day. Instead, he arranged for his buddy who owned the town taxi service to give me a ride. The taxi service consisted of one cab and a short white handicapped-accessible van. That morning, the cab was on a call, so Dad's friend pulled up to the motel in what to my horror was now my private little school bus and told me to hop aboard. The van had been in a minor accident that rendered the passenger door inoperable, so I had to climb in via the wheelchair ramp. I could already see the odds of a Danny Zuko-esque first day appearance fading quickly.

"I'll drop you off out front," my oblivious driver cheerfully said as we turned onto the street where my new school awaited.

"No, no, you don't have to do that. Just stop here, it's fine," I suggested a good block away.

"It's no trouble at all! Your dad's a friend!" he insisted. By then, we were pulling up to the curb right in front of all the students filing off their not-so-short buses. I could feel everyone stop to stare as the ramp noisily lowered and I started to walk down it. I didn't even make it to the sidewalk before the first flying Coke can hit me in the side of the head.

It was a harsh reminder that kids could be cruel, but I was determined to endure, and salvage what dignity I could. I picked up the can and made the long shot into the trash (this was a LONG time before recycling programs), then went inside. Within no time, I overheard some kids by my locker talking about magic. They had a pack of playing cards . . . and I was in.

Who knew—after years of harassing him for being a nerdy magician, it would actually save his reputation?

You were president of the Crime Stoppers Club, you ran unopposed, and there was no crime to stop. Exactly. I was that good.

I would talk on the phone to Drew at least every other day. He would fill me in on everything I was missing out on, and I would paint the bitter picture of my isolation in High River. The school hadn't been updated since students wrote on stone tablets and ate woolly mammoth burgers for lunch. It had none of the brand-new amenities or high-tech bells and whistles that Thomas Haney Secondary boasted back in Maple Ridge. Worst of all was the complete loss of autonomy. *Adios*, open schedules and independent learning plans. Gone, too, were the myriad extracurricular activities I was involved in, like theater and coaching, not to mention all the important offices I held.

The bottom line was that I had just transferred from Oz to Alcatraz.

My school day dragged out minute by dull minute for what felt like 17 hours until the final bell. It was deflating to sit in a cell-like classroom again and plod over material at a snail's pace. Boredom had never been a factor for me before, but now, without enough juice to fully charge, my brain powered down like a phone on airplane mode. (Yeah, I know smartphones weren't invented yet, but who wants to compare their brain to a Walkman on dead batteries?)

I felt like the life and lust for learning were being sucked right out of me. I went from straight-As to getting Ds for the first time in my life. What the HECK was happening? And how was I going to salvage my GPA when there was no option to make whimsical short films for extra credit? It would've taken a remake of *Titanic* and a Golden Globe nomination just to raise History to a measly C-plus.

At least the house was going well, though. Dad and I got it framed in good time despite the challenge of brutal prairie winds that blew me right off the scaffolding. I wasn't hurt, and no flying monkeys showed up, but Drew and Pedro did (which was close enough), and just in time.

My classmates had stopped lobbing Coke cans at my head once I gained acceptance as the guy who could do cool magic tricks and deliver some good one-liners, but those new friendships couldn't offer the kind of support I needed at the moment. That kind of reassurance only comes with friends who not only know your whole back story but also lived it with you.

Drew and Pedro weren't there just to boost my sagging spirits, though. They were our free day laborers to do the grunt work while Dad and I handled the precision surgery, like gluing and nailing the knotty pine wood cladding on the vaulted ceilings in our living room.

Mind you, I'm not dissing either one of them here. Pedro was especially good with welding and any mechanical problems—his uncles owned an auto-repair shop where he had practically grown up, and he could rebuild an entire engine by himself in less than a day. And much as I like to tease him, Drew has an incredible work ethic and won't stop until he's mastered whatever is at hand.* He and Pedro made a great problem-solving team—no question there. It was the no-brainer stuff that tripped them up.

Digging a simple hole, for example. (Here is where I'm dissing them.)

Drew and Pedro were assigned the task of shoveling an outhouse hole 5 feet deep and about 3 feet across. They dug away all afternoon. They were like possessed chipmunks. When they were done, they were very,

*PAID ANNOUNCEMENT

Drew

Jonathan

WE HAD OUR OWN MEANS
OF HORSEPOWER TO GET AROUND.

-Jonathan

very proud that they had dug the perfect hole. Yep, it was exactly the size it was supposed to be.

Too bad it was in the wrong place. Chip 'n' Dale had dug a latrine where a fence post was supposed to go. This was why Dad always used to say, "This is more a Jon thing" when something broke around the house and Drew started jumping up and down begging him, "Let me fix it, Dad! I can fix it!"

With tenth grade at an end, I realized I was going to have to kick major butt to get my grades back up if I planned on earning a degree more advanced than my certificate from Parks and Rec clown college. And if I was going to win a scholarship, which I needed, I would have to earn straight As my junior and senior years. Returning to Maple Ridge and my old high school was my best shot at doing that. Dad would stay behind to finish the house, hiring help as needed. Mom would bring all three of us boys back to Alberta on school breaks to pitch in.

Just like our father with his cowboy aspirations, Drew and I had both been lucky enough to discover our calling early on. For Drew, that was acting and athletics.

My all-consuming passion, of course, was for magic. I was maybe 12 years old when I met my first real magician at our city's outdoor New Year's Eve celebration. His name was David Wilson and he was going from person to person doing tricks and making people laugh. I was so mesmerized by his effects that I started trailing him around the party, watching intently and asking a million questions. I was totally hooked. I devoured every book, video, TV special, and live performance I could in a quest to become the next David Copperfield. Preferably by age 13.

While you mostly just acted athletic.

So your idea to rig the lottery by buying 10,000 tickets counts as one of your good plans, right? Details, details.

As similar as we seem, Drew and I were actually polar opposites when it came to how we approached our shared love of performing. As an actor, what Drew wanted most was for people to see the truth he brought to each role. As a magician, my aim was to deliver thrills by deceiving the hell out of them. Even though our creative paths diverged, Drew and I still had the same destination: center stage.

We were also raised to understand that we'd never get there by just forging blindly ahead.

One of the advantages of doing most everything in tandem growing up is that practically nothing ever happened in a vacuum. We had to routinely consult, compromise, cooperate, and conspire with each other, so working out a plan became second nature. That's not to say they were all *good* plans, but the habit wasn't a bad one to have.

Striking out on our own at 18, with different careers in mind, it didn't occur to us to each just go our separate way and find our own success. The question at hand was how we could combine forces and create enough momentum to propel both of us to the top.

We both enrolled in the University of Calgary, which allowed us a little freedom while staying within reasonable striking distance of the ranch in case we needed some Mom and Dad time. I ended up getting a full academic scholarship, and declared a major in business with a minor in theater design. I wanted to be well prepared to run every aspect of my own touring show as a magician, from the finances and growth strategy to the staging requirements like lighting, rigging, and drafting. I even managed to turn a group project in one class into a conveniently self-serving blueprint for my future. We were supposed

JONATHAN: We are always on the same page. It's like having that best friend who can finish your sentences, times 1,000. Drew can even START my sentences.

DREW: If I had a dollar for every crazy, ridiculous, absurd scheme Jonathan came up with . . . I'd have a lot more money to invest in every one of them.

to choose a business, then create a plan, showing research, statistics, and everything else we'd need to work out to launch it. Other groups were doing things like a laundromat or coffee shop, but our team slayed with "The Magic of Jonathan Silver" touring show. I was so fixated on that goal, I could have converted "The Magic of Jonathan Silver" into credit in marine science if needed.

Drew was even more obsessed with basketball. Coming to Calgary with an athletic scholarship, he studied kinesiology so he could earn a living in sports beyond the career he hoped for on the court. He wanted to be a high school coach eventually, but in Canada, coaches don't get paid: Teachers volunteer after school. Drew needed the kinesiology degree so he could teach health and phys ed. What he wanted in the immediate future, though, was to make U Calgary's basketball team.

On top of our chosen fields, we were still keen to keep making our short indie films and immerse ourselves more in that creative world. We had made our first very short film in eleventh grade. It was called *A Summer Affair*, which was something our 16-year-old selves had zero direct knowledge of, but limitless interest in.

The film was a very greased-lightning type of production following a boy and girl in high school who were destined to fall in love but didn't realize their passion for each other was mutual. Drew played the guy and I directed. Even though it was a tad cheesy, it was pretty hilarious. Or at least we thought so. It was filled with inside jokes that only our group of friends would really understand, but everyone else still laughed enough for us to deem it a success.

After college, we started shooting other short films on shoestring budgets. One of my favorites is *Karma Inc.*, a dark comedy that stirred a lot of buzz in the independent scene. It's about this otherworldly office that manages all the karma on earth. I played the head of the negative karma division, and Drew was of course head of the positive side. Another one, called *A Better Me*, played off of the typical stereotypes that you would find at the gym and questioned why some people are so obsessed with feeling better on the outside instead of diving deeper into the problems that exist on the inside.

We were resourceful, and could usually keep our budget under a couple thousand dollars, though *Karma Inc.* broke the bank at ten thousand. We would beg, borrow, and steal (well, no grand theft larceny) to pay for these productions, which not surprisingly weren't making us any money in return. We just did it because we loved telling stories, making people laugh, and more importantly, making people think.

We would dip into money we made from our early house flips and a LOT of random jobs to fund our filmmaking and other interests, like Drew's sock collection.

We worked at a mid-sized mall. Our uniforms had this belt loaded down with all these attachments that looked very official. In truth we were only issued pepper spray, handcuffs, and a notepad. Drew was actually the supervisor, so he was all about finding ways to make the schedule more efficient.

We're both pretty social, and while on foot patrol through those mean streets that smelled perpetually of fresh cinnamon rolls, we liked

a) That was much later and, b) "mall cop" is more of a calling than a job. Are unsupervised juveniles walking up the down escalator? Book 'em, Danno!

Drew

Jonathan

IF THERE WAS AN ADVENTURE TO BE FOUND . . .
WE WOULD FIND IT. IF NONE EXISTED,
WE'D DREAM IT UP.
-Jonathan

(not us)

popping into the different shops to chat with the employees. That came to a (possibly screaming) halt after complaints about one of the creepy security guards prompted the mall to ban any of us from going into the stores.

There were several occasions when we arrested people, but we didn't have a mall jail, so we made them wait in the office until the real police arrived. Usually it was just shoplifters or kids who were vandalizing, but we also would get perverts trying to streak through the mall. If you've ever had to handcuff someone with no clothes on, then you know that it's a little disconcerting.

We had equally colorful, fleeting careers as busboys, waiters, valet (Drew), shoe salesman (go ahead, look at our feet and take a guess), personal trainer/cougar bait (Drew again), and website designer/ computer geek (me).

I'd like to say we killed at whatever job undertook, but the record will show that Drew was the absolute worst waiter. He would talk to his tables for so long that he would forget to put their orders in, including one time when it was twenty people having a celebration of some kind.

I, on the other hand, mastered the art of service. I worked in a restaurant called Red Robin, and could take on a double section more effectively than other waiters struggling with a single four top. I would do balloon animals for kids, magic for special occasions, and could

Haha, I would convince them their meal took extra time because it was special.

"We're sorry. We're waiting for the chicken to lay your eggs." When they asked me to consider being a host instead . . . I just considered another career path.

Is collecting phone numbers considered working?

always make my diners laugh. I made far more in tips than I ever made in wages. Not that it was anywhere near as rewarding as the time I worked in a women's swimwear store.

When we were in third grade, Drew and I would get pulled out of class a few times a week and were put into a special program where they were introducing kids to computers. We had those original block-like Apple Macintoshes, and they taught us not only how to use them, but how to program. I thought it was the coolest thing in the world and have been very into computers ever since. In college, I took a few courses on graphic/web design, and I had a few side jobs building computers, designing websites, and doing graphic work.

One of my clients was a swim store that hired me to design their website. The owner was so impressed, he asked me to design the posters and banners for inside the store, too. Then he mentioned that one of his stores wasn't doing so well, and before I knew it, he asked if I would be interested in managing it. I gave it careful thought for approximately two seconds. Running a bikini shop was a no-brainer. LOL.

I took over the business, created some sales events, and really managed to turn it around. I had no complaints about helping the women who wanted a second opinion on the swimwear they were trying on. Perk of the job. But once I hired new staff and turned the store around, I moved on. Bikini Boss was just a small project for very selfish reasons, but as far as I was concerned, not a career commitment.

Drew got his own eyeful when he took a job at a gym as a personal trainer, but he was more traumatized than tantalized by it.

It was basically just women with money to burn that wanted a young guy to fondle them. I mean, who shows up at the gym in full makeup, prom hair, and a thong?!

Luckily, since Drew was going to need lots of therapy, my knowledge of the web and where it was going led to a brand-new moneymaker for me. I teamed up with a buddy of mine to create a business where we would buy domains and sell them for profit. This was hard for people to wrap their brains around because there was no physical asset. But we were successfully turning many domains around, and developing a lot of websites. I saw an opportunity to get into web hosting.

Everybody who has a website or email has to host it somewhere, and I had worked out a system where I could undercut the bigger players and offer much more. I had hundreds of clients in the blink of an eye. The business was called $10 Hosting, which was ironic because my product only cost $7.77 a month.

The marketing was slick, the product was solid, but at the end of the day it was too hard to convince the masses that they should go with a small independent provider. When other companies started offering drastically reduced hosting that was ad-supported, it was time to get out. I managed to sell the business for a reasonable profit and began to focus more energy on the flips Drew and I were doing. No matter how many other jobs we cycled through, real estate still held our interest and allowed us to keep chasing our biggest dreams.

And we had every reason to believe we would catch them, as long as we were willing to work hard and stayed true to ourselves.

Proof of that could be found on an Alberta horse ranch in the shadow of the Canadian Rockies, where a pair of dreamers we knew chased theirs with a station wagon full of kids until they finally found the perfect place to park.

WE DON'T COMPETE TO KNOCK EACH OTHER DOWN.
WE COMPETE TO PUSH EACH OTHER TO DO BETTER.
-Jonathan

Comments by Jonathan

BROTHER VS. BROTHER

When Jonathan and I were small, there wasn't really an obvious sign of rivalry between us. Mom fondly remembers how we developed a system for sharing toys before we could even speak. If I wanted a turn playing with whatever Jonathan was busy with, I would reach over and give his hair a light tug. He would hand me the toy, find something else to play with, then tug my hair when he wanted something I had. No tears or tantrums. We were very chill little rugrats. Over time, Mom recalls that a revolving sense of tot-tatorship emerged where we each would become "the boss" for a couple of weeks. Then flip for the other one to take control. It happened like clockwork, as though there were a hidden calendar under our cribs, and it lasted for a couple of years.

That continued to evolve after we discovered karate at the age of 6 and our competitive streak came knocking. We let it in and have been feeding it ever since. Jonathan, JD, and I all took lessons at the local dojo, where our father served as a senior instructor assisting the sensei. Dad was already a black belt, and with a houseful of rowdy boys to wrangle, he was counting on the ancient wisdom of the martial arts to instill some self-discipline in us. We were counting on it as a free pass to kick and karate chop each other.

We excelled at karate and were flying up the ranks in no time. We created our own little contests to see who could master new combinations first or beat the other in a little hand-to-hand combat. The goal was to get good enough to enter local—and eventually national—tournaments. It took around a year's worth of lessons and practice at home before we were deemed ready to pit our skills against other junior Jean-Claude van Damme wannabes. Jonathan and I especially liked to use each other to attempt JCVD's signature kick to an opponent's head while doing a 360-degree turn midair—which, for the record, was not part of the sequence of moves 8-year-olds were expected to exhibit at a kids' karate tournament. No matter. We just wanted to bring honor to our dojo by proving it was the top dojo in the entire world, which we assumed had heard of Maple Ridge and was watching intently to see what we would achieve next.

We all feared you would take your ninja skills, defect to the Cobra Kai, and torment the world as an evil karate villain.

The tournaments were broken down into three sections—kumite, kata, and team kata. Kumite, which means something like "grappling hands" in Japanese, is sparring or fighting. Kata refers to form, and competitors are judged by how well they execute different combinations of jumps, kicks, and air punches. In team kata, Jonathan and I usually paired up with our sensei's son to face down rival dojos, and more often than not we took home the gold.

Karate was the first sport we got into, and it was fun to start at zero and be able to see our practice pay off as we grew stronger and more agile. I'm the type of person who's always liked clarity and order. Physical challenges appeal to me for the same reason math does: Once you understand each factor clearly, you can reach the logical outcome. There aren't any maybes after an equals sign. We trained in karate at least three times a week, forgoing other after-school activities and playtime with our school friends to get as good at karate as we possibly could. I didn't want *a* gold medal. I wanted gold in everything I tried.

At the end of every tournament, much to my annoyance, it almost always came down to the same two finalists squaring off against each other in kumite and kata.

Jonathan and me.

Since kata is a solo demonstration of technique, scored by judges in an Olympic figure-skating fashion, there was always a clear winner . . . and much to my chagrin, that was usually Jonathan.

With kumite, things got confusing. For starters, the judges couldn't tell us apart until someone got the idea of putting ribbons on us. Like tagging wolves being reintroduced to the wild. Or flagging a tree to cut down. Typically I wore a white ribbon and Jonathan sported red, and once the judges had that sorted out, I could rightfully claim the

Yeah, I think I pulled a hammy that day!

victory that was mine almost every time. There should have been a medal above gold for that, because sparring with your identical twin is like fighting your own image in the mirror. We knew each other's every move and could not only anticipate them, but replicate them.

Even though we each had a forte—and a gold medal to call our own—I still wanted to beat Jonathan in kata in the worst way. It did happen once in a while, and Jonathan likewise beat me at kumite if I was having a really off day, like fighting off smallpox or something. I didn't want to just win an occasional match, though, and I didn't want to defeat Jonathan to tear him down. (To save face, I touted a half-baked theory about our skill levels actually being equal, "it's just that I have a slightly different technique.") I knew he was considered the best at kata, so I wanted to hit that mark, then edge past and become a *better* best.

That held true in everything, not just karate. When we were in high school, we were both straight-A students. But if Jonathan had a 98% in English and I had a 95%, that three-point difference would light a fire in me to study that much harder the following quarter. I didn't want my future obituary to read: *Acclaimed Oscar-winning filmmaker and actor Drew Scott, who got an A-minus in English in the 11th grade, finally died of abject shame Thursday at the age of 102.*

Obviously the two of us were cast from the same overachiever mold, and I don't think there was a time in our adult lives when we weren't trying to outdo each other in something. JD swears it's genetically

He is survived by his twin brother, Jonathan, who gets to live longer and die happier because he achieved a higher score in the same class.

Your eyes instantly bugged out of your head, the tears started streaming, and you dumped a full bottle of Coca-Cola on your tongue. Still can't believe you actually did it.

imprinted in us to always achieve the next level. I'm not sure whether he's implying that his younger brothers are cloned genius bots from a distant galaxy, or that we're just too stupid to stop ourselves half the time. Sometimes what gets us going is just a harmless (*Curious George and the Icy Hill and the Superfast Toboggan Race*) sense of mischief. Sometimes it's not as harmless as we thought (*Curious George and the Icy Hill and the Superfast Toboggan Race and the Barbed Wire Fence Just Past the Finish Line*). Torn clothes and blood in the snow only served to make the contest more exciting; we only had about 10 feet between the finish line and the fence o'death to bail off the sleds. Defeat hurt worse. That same philosophy applied the time Jonathan dared me to shoot an entire bottle of Tabasco sauce.

Victory requires sacrifice. My taste buds understand that and don't miss the ability to identify flavor.

On the horse ranch where we grew up, we would challenge each other in cowboy competitions, like seeing who could saddle a horse the fastest and make it across the finish line first. One time, we each grabbed a horse, threw a blanket and saddle on its back, jumped on, and loped toward the finish line. I was in the lead when I felt my saddle slip—I hadn't cinched it up tight enough. Before I knew it, the saddle (with me still in it) had slid completely under the still-galloping horse. All I could do was hang on for dear life between the horse's moving legs. (*WHOA!* is not a command a horse readily responds to from someone riding its belly.)

I still won the race, though.

JONATHAN: Is it really a competition when I win the majority of the time?

DREW: Fact check, everybody knows that "history" is written by the winner, and I've been giving you history lessons my whole life.

We'd also race each other climbing massive evergreens at the edge of the forest bordering our farm. The fact that it never crossed our minds as to how incredibly dangerous it was is a complete mystery, because the branches were perpetually slick from the frequent rain or the morning dew. On the rare occasion where we did slip and tumble a good 30 feet, the dozens of bushy boughs below would break the fall and slow us down enough to prevent any broken bones. Then we'd simply brush off and climb again. I'm assuming the light blows to the head prevented us from learning the error of our ways.

If we weren't testing our speed at something, it was only because we were temporarily distracted by the nagging question—asked only by us—of who was more flexible. Jonathan decided he could settle the debate and prove he was a human Gumby by sliding two desks together in our classroom and doing the splits between them. He was already at maximum wishbone when one of the desks slipped and he pulled a groin muscle. For the next couple of weeks, he walked like a kid desperately in need of a bathroom break, with his knees locked together in some kind of toddler shuffle. That didn't stop us from concocting other ridiculous competitions.

Adulthood didn't stop us, either.

If you ask our best buddy of 25 years to describe the most idiotic thing we've ever turned into a competition, Pedro will claim we shut our arms in the door of a bathroom cubicle to see who could last the longest. I could see Pedro and Jonathan doing this, but personally I wouldn't choose a public toilet stall for any kind of showdown. Jona-

Then I guess "I" win the bruised forearm and surface germ competitions!

than, on the other hand, has been documented wiping his finger across a dirty chandelier and licking it. He's disgusting. Which isn't to say I haven't been party to an embarrassing contest or two—just not this particular one.

My vote for one of the dumbest was during high school, when we both started developing pain in our knuckles and these weird little lumps on the backs of our hands. Could hands even get the mumps? Since it happened to us simultaneously, a reasonable assumption would be that it was genetic, right? The mysterious lumps seemed to pulse with pain, and we waited for the moment when aliens would burst out and Sigourney Weaver would have to save us. But then . . . a moment of moronic clarity.

"That's vein damage," the doctor instantly concluded. Had the backs of our hands been subjected to some kind of repeat trauma? We decided not to mention the aliens attempting to escape. Besides, we had a pretty good hunch now what caused our swollen veins: A unique form of intense hand-to-hand combat designed to test a man's grit, reflexes, brute strength, and . . . idiocy.

It was a game called Knuckles. It's sort of like slap-jack using a closed fist and no cards. You stand fist to fist with your opponent, then on the word "GO!" you take turns hitting each other in the knuckles on the back of the other person's hand. The opponent can't flinch if you fake a hit. Three flinches and the other player gets a free hit. You play until someone can't take the pain anymore and surrenders. Jonathan and I played Knuckles obsessively with all of our closest friends at school. The winner never won anything. Pride was the only thing at stake. Pride being relative once you've had to admit to a medical professional that you have a Knuckles problem and you and your brother like to see who can deliver the greatest number of sharp, painful knuckle raps to the other in rapid succession.

Don't judge. It's a thing—check the Internet. In Russia, it's a blood sport.

This is the part where it would make sense to just blame our parents for everything. We wouldn't even have to throw them under the bus—they'd wait patiently at the bus stop, flag it down, and hurl themselves beneath the wheels for us if need be. Actually, they're so supportive that they'd probably do it for total strangers, too. The ONLY thing that gave me that single-tear feeling of temporary parental abandonment is that I can't recall Mom and Dad ever actually attending one of my high school basketball games. My point is, we never felt like we had to vie for their attention, and they didn't send us to bed without dinner when MIT didn't recruit us by age 9. Or ever.

What they also didn't do was pretend that just showing up was the same as breaking a sweat, or that your best was *the* best as long as you tried. Participation leagues may have good intentions in declaring everyone a winner, but they end up teaching kids it's not alright to fail. Sometimes people are afraid to fail, and we all lose if smart, creative minds aren't encouraged to take risks. I remember when we had Track and Field Day in the eighth grade, and the teacher was signing everybody up for different events.

"Who wants to do the 100-meter dash?" he asked.

Most everybody's hand shot up, including Jonathan's, which I

Strange, 'cause they always came to my magic performances. Because they were hoping to finally witness your disappearance.

thought was strange because he hated running. The teacher picked the first kid he saw.

"The 200-meter?"

Everybody who didn't get on the 100-meter list tried again, but only one was picked.

By the time it came to the 400-meter, enthusiasm had dwindled and only the avid racers were still volunteering at this point . . . oh, and Jonathan.

"Okay, who wants to run the 1,500-meter?"

Then, as if the jogging gods were dishing out hilarious retribution for me, Jonathan's was the only hand that went up.

The teacher put his name down before he had a chance to re-evaluate the critical error he had made. And in this class, once your name was down, you couldn't take it back.

Running wasn't Jonathan's thing. If it had been hurdles or any jumping event, I wouldn't have been surprised: One of our favorite pastimes at home was to set up high jumps in one of the fields by putting poles between trash cans. We piled up sleeping bags to use as a landing mat. Dad's good Arctic one designed to withstand the cold at 40-below was nice and thick, and since we'd never known him to set off for the tundra to spend the winter hunting polar bears, we were pretty sure he wouldn't notice it was missing. We actually ranked in the top five in high school for high jump, and in the top ten district-wide. Why Jonathan thought his ability to jump like a kangaroo counted as training to run a mile is baffling, but then again, a lot of what Jonathan thinks and does falls into that category.

Jonathan approached his medium-distance race the same as a

I'm an enigma wrapped in a riddle. And plaid.

TOGETHER WE STAND,
DIVIDED WE PLACE 8TH
IN THE 1500 METER.
SERIOUSLY, NEVER LETTING
THAT GO.
-Drew

Hey! Everybody knows I came in 8th. Sounds pretty awesome to me.

Not when there are only 8 people in the race!

sprint, assuming, since he had no training whatsoever for the event, that you just take off and keep running as fast as you can to the finish line. As he failed to pace himself, what started off strong quickly began to falter, as one by one every other racer passed him. He came in dead last, lungs burning and muscles screaming. Our teacher gave him a hero's welcome at the finish line. "It was a GREAT try, Jonathan! You did GREAT! Next time will be even better!" Dad was waiting at the finish line, too. He looked at the overly optimistic teacher and said with his typical deadpan, understated honesty:

"You came in last."

Dad was a straight-shooting cowboy, and he didn't see how building false pride was going to build character. It wasn't meant to be cruel; it was just a little dose of brutal honesty, which is much funnier to recant now than it was to experience then. If you're going to have a competition, then the kudos belong to whoever proves himself or herself best. We were raised to respect that simple fact of life, and it didn't make us feel worthless if we didn't happen to merit the gold medal or blue ribbon that day. Envious, maybe, but it was a good hunger to have.

One of the biggest differences between Jonathan and me is that I probably would have treated that 1,500-meter loss as a gauntlet thrown and knocked myself out for the next year trying to become Usain Bolt. Jonathan didn't spend that kind of energy just to see how good he could get at something he didn't care passionately enough about in the first place.

Our karate dojo was always looking for ways to raise money for

It felt like we were hustling for cattle rustlers, selling chuck roast door-to-door.

trips and tournaments, and one time, our sensei decided that we should sell butchered cuts of meat.

As incentive, the sensei announced that whoever raised the most money for the fundraiser would get a very special prize: two authentic Japanese swords. A Katana and a Samurai, with watermarked blades. "*Swords?*" Jonathan and I did a Scooby-Doo impersonation in unison. We already had a sword addiction, and these two beauties belonged in our collection! We needed to sit down and strategize.

"Okay," I told Jonathan, "there are two of us, but we share the same market, so we should pool whatever we make under one name instead of splitting up." We didn't know it then, but "divide and conquer" would become a critical key to our success one day. For now, it was just the best shot at getting our hands on those swords.

We hit the ground running. We may have been kids, but we were seasoned pros at sales already from our hanger business and the infamous Kimo Blasters. We charmed, pressured, and outright begged every relative and family friend we could to stock their freezers with a side of beef. We rang bells and were happily surprised by how many people were willing to buy frozen veal chops from some random kid on their doorstep. We wanted those swords so bad, we would have started selling whole cows door-to-door if we could. Anything to increase revenue.

When the fundraiser was over, we won by a landslide. We were ecstatic. We already had the spot picked out on our bedroom wall to display the swords. Then the sensei said that since our dad was an assistant instructor, our family was part of the dojo, so the prize

Did Frazier remind Ali?

was given to one of the other kids! We couldn't believe what we were hearing. The amount of money we had brought in was so far over and above the runner-up, we could have divided it by the two of us and we still would have clearly been on top. We were devastated. Dad was furious and volunteered himself to defend our honor. He marched down to the dojo and confronted the master. Our sensei didn't realize how important this was to us and what was an innocent mistake was quickly rectified when he bought a second set of swords to award to us. There was balance in the universe again and we were over the moon.

When you're an identical twin, it's only natural to want to distinguish yourself somehow, and for me, sports was the surefire way to do that. I dominated in all of them save for wrestling (no technique, I just picked opponents up and slammed them down like Bamm-Bamm from *The Flintstones*) and tetherball (Jonathan forgot to remind me about the tournament).

And Ping-Pong.

I was good at Ping-Pong. Very good, even. But Jonathan was unbeatable, and it drove me fifty shades of crazy that no matter how good my game got, it never improved enough to win consistently against him. Did the Peter Principle apply to Ping-Pong? Had I risen to the level of my incompetence smashing a tiny ball over a 6-inch net? Jonathan probably had some advantage I couldn't figure out up his magic sleeve. I'd fallen victim to his sleight of hand in Monopoly marathons before ("How did my race car suddenly turn into an iron again?") I needed to confront this Ping-Pong paradox like the baller I was. It was time to call in the ~~big guns~~. *little paddles*

I did some research and found William, a Ping-Pong ninja from

Toronto, to coach me. He was my Miyagi, and graciously agreed to take on my sad case. I would play and learn several times a week with him. For the first couple of months, he wanted to break my years of bad habits. It was the *Karate Kid* equivalent of painting fences. He clearly was not grasping how urgent this was. I needed to beat Jonathan *now*, not at the senior center when we were 80. William decided to spend the next couple of months training me on patience. AHHHHH! I didn't have time for that. But William's philosophy did have merit. He said the goal in table tennis is to play defense and wait for the perfect set-up, or for your opponent to mess up. That was the beginning of my real training and what transformed my whole game. After six grueling months, I was finally trusted with my first secret weapon. The spin!! Jonathan would have no choice but to bow before me—I was ready to pull off a Ping-Pong coup and overthrow the champ. Jonathan and I set the time and a date that it would all go down. We did up a UFC-worthy graphic and distributed it to our friends. We did every-thing except sell tickets (which, in hindsight, would have been a great revenue opportunity).

I had practiced with William for what seemed like an eternity. This was the moment I had been waiting for all these months. It was the culmination of all that hard work, countless late nights, and a massive investment in pro gear. We stepped up to the table, gave each other a nod, and the first ball dropped.

The first game took less than five minutes, and in some bizarro turn of events, Jonathan destroyed me, 11–6. What the holy hell?!!! I quickly learned I had been training with a pro who knew how he was supposed to return the ball. Jonathan knew nothing—he was the idiot savant of Ping-Pong—and it was messing with my mojo!

Drew insists on keeping score even in mini-golf. I change the numbers just to mess with him.

"Best two out of three," I declared. And though I won the second game, Jonathan rebounded for the third and hence maintained his title.

I wanted to break my custom paddle, but I had paid $280 for it and had grown quite fond of it. I took a sabbatical from the circuit and went back to training. After the rematch six months later, it was official . . . I was unbeatable, as long as I had my good paddle.

Friends who know us both well cite my personal Ping-Pong trainer as proof that I can't bear to lose and am uber-competitive about everything. While I wouldn't dispute that *entirely*, I have to say at the end of the day that it's more about challenging myself than Jonathan. We push each other to do better, not to get out of the way. It's funny, but we've never established a clear-cut twin hierarchy; we're both alpha personalities, and we just sort of instinctively pass the baton back and forth for the leadership role at any given time. Flashback to toddlerhood when Mom said we did the exact same thing. Maybe old habits die . . . old? And it's not like we have matured much after all these years.

We both have our perfectionist tendencies, but mine runs so deep I try to perfect my perfectionism. I always like to be doing something; if we're at the beach, I want to be playing volleyball or jet-skiing or trying some new sport. I can't just lie in the sand. I'm always up for a new activity, but I don't want to be bad at it. I like taking lessons because my philosophy is, "Why reinforce bad habits when you can learn to do it right?" It's true, I'm sort of a lesson-holic. The list is long, but for

Mmm, big fan of a beachside lounge and a nap.

starters, besides Ping-Pong, I've taken guitar, singing, voice, hip-hop dancing, volleyball, golf, parkour, cooking, trapeze, and Spanish. I was better at trapeze than Spanish, but I haven't given up on the latter. I would get better faster if they awarded vintage Toledo swords for conjugating irregular verbs.

We had been doing *Property Brothers* for a couple of years when HGTV realized there was gold in pushing our competitive buttons, so we created a series pitting us head-to-head against each other in the ultimate flipping showdown. For the first two seasons of *Brother vs. Brother*, we each mentored a team of five people who wanted to be the next big thing in design/construction. The weakest contestant would be eliminated challenge by challenge until we declared a winner. Since our primary role was just to guide our teams, I knew going in that I had the advantage over Jonathan—I'd originally aspired to be a PE teacher and had done a ton of coaching while in high school and college. Jonathan couldn't even teach Stewie where the doggie door was when he was a puppy; Gracie, the older pooch, finally got exasperated with Stewie's yapping and did Jonathan's job for him. I easily won the first two seasons of *BvB*.

In the third season, we took *Brother vs. Brother* in-house and began to produce it ourselves. The original format had been costly to produce, and because it was an elimination challenge, the show didn't have an afterlife in reruns. We scrapped the idea of mentoring teams of amateurs and turned the show into a head-to-head competition in flipping. We would each be responsible for buying, renovating, and selling a fixer-upper. I did my own design and oversaw my own construction

Are you taking credit for a contestant's victory?

so there was no way Jonathan could contest future losses. When the houses were done, we listed them, and the brother who made the most profit in the end would win. Jonathan won Season 3, so I came into Season 4 determined to reclaim my title. Jonathan won again.

That meant that Season 5 would be the tiebreaker. We went to Galveston, Texas, and boiled down dozens of houses with potential to our top contenders. We each had a budget of $600,000. I got a run-down house on a canal for $335,000, but so many major structural problems were uncovered during inspection, I was able to negotiate it down to $275,000, which left me $325,000 for the renovation. I was likely to need every penny. The house was going to be a beast to flip, but I purposely chose the worst one I saw. I was tired of losing to Jonathan, and I knew I needed to go big or go home.

I know I can make a house pretty, and I know Jonathan can make a house pretty, so I was going to have to be very strategic in how I played this.

One of the biggest misconceptions people have is that I'm strictly a real estate agent who never gets his hands dirty. But I started designing, renovating, and flipping houses in the mid-1990s—right out of high school, same as Jonathan. I may not have the construction and design education or experience that Jonathan has today, and unlike him, I definitely hate getting unidentifiable sludge under my nails. But because I work every day buying and selling homes, I know what adds value, I know where to spend money so it counts, and I know exactly what buyers want. Jonathan can't claim that.

I'm also very calculating. For *BvB* Season 5, I spoke with HOAs, other real estate agents, and people who lived in the area to figure out what type of buyers were coming to Galveston. I quickly realized the large majority were investors looking for rental properties. That meant my potential buyers would want "heads in beds," meaning I had to fit as many beds as comfortably possible in this place so the investor-owners could ask for higher rents.

Right smack in the middle of the already cramped kitchen was a tiki hut straight out of *Gilligan's Island*. Taking that tiki hut down turned out to be a maddening chore: It looked like one good puff of air would blow the whole palm-fronded thing down, but no such luck. Even harder to get rid of was the indoor rock-climbing wall that stood strong against the sledgehammer assault for an impressive amount of time. Then there was a huge, ugly, ten-person hot tub upstairs in the master bedroom, which left me wondering what kind of parties they were having in this place. Outside, a big pergola was going to get demolished, too. Every one of the eyesores proved surprisingly resilient. I had the feeling the whole sagging house could fall down, but that damn rock wall and tiki hut would still be standing in the ruins.

The house was held up by stilts, and on a day with a particularly low water level, I happened to be looking down at the shallow canal and noticed one of the pilings looked rotted almost all the way through. It turned out that there was some bug that eats away at the wood underwater—a termite in scuba gear, apparently—and every piling had been nibbled away to practically nothing. They were all going to have to be replaced, but doing so would take a feat of engineering that was definitely outside my wheelhouse and commandeered a big chunk out of my cash reserve. I was beginning to wonder what I'd gotten myself into. At least I had been able to carve two extra bedrooms out of the unwieldy master closet and an equally cavernous laundry room. I now had a five-bedroom house on the water. More beds for more heads. I sent a drone up the canal to spy on Jonathan and see what his house was looking like. In real-time I could see he had installed a beautiful window wall across the entire south side of the living room. He must have stolen my idea, as I wanted to do the same thing but didn't have the budget. But structural repairs had cost me a fortune already, and I knew Jonathan didn't have nearly as bad a hand as I'd dealt myself.

But I stood by my philosophy that I had to be bold. This was Texas, and I had to go big. As my budget ballooned and my profit margin shrank, I maintained my game face, even though inside I was absolutely dying. If by some chance Jonathan pulled off the holy trinity of home-flipping wins, I would be crushed for good. This was the proverbial straw that would break this camo-print-wearing agent's back. Renovations complete, the houses were listed and my fate was officially in the hands of the buyer. It was touch-and-go until the very end.

I finally won, and it was a landslide.

That was a spin shot Jonathan never saw coming.

PLATO SAID THE FIRST
AND BEST VICTORY IS
TO CONQUER SELF. CLEARLY HE
DIDN'T HAVE A TWIN.
-Drew

THE GRAND DREAMS and underhanded schemes you see on *Brother vs. Brother* are nothing compared to family game night in our living room. Here's how to turn an innocent board game into a marathon death match.

Strategy
Drew: Make sure you control the bank. Start slow, buy a couple of choice properties, and invest in putting up hotels until you've recreated the Las Vegas Strip on a single lot.
Jonathan: Get in the market fast and buy up all of the cheapest properties until you dominate an entire half of the board. The up-front cost is huge, but you can take out a second mortgage later.

Downfall
Drew: My magical nemesis is *so* predictable, and always ends up broke or in jail, where he's stuck with empty rooms he can't collect rent on while I wander in circles by myself, waiting for him to post bail or roll out.

Jonathan: Jail is a much better option than the crushing financial misstep of landing on your overdeveloped mega-monstrosities. Oh, and I should be able to rezone for a strip mall of bail bondsmen. And while we're at it, what's the point of Marvin having a garden if I can't up the rent by adding on a sweet deck with a wood-burning pizza oven?

Alleged Desperate Measures

Drew: Hide cash in off-shore accounts. Baffle with complex negotiations that inevitably result in acceptance over mental exhaustion. Never turn down the opportunity to stash extra bills embezzled from another friend's board.

Jonathan: Create an open-concept jail by demo'ing exterior wall. Add tiny houses to trains on money-losing railroad and call them sleeper cars to collect more rent. Use magic skills to vanish a few of your archrival's hotels. Or your archrival.

WHEN I WAS A
CHILD, THE WORLD
WAS FILLED WITH
MAGIC AND MYSTERY.
I JUST DECIDED TO
KEEP IT THAT WAY.
—Jonathan

David Copperfield

SMOKE AND MIRRORS

L ike a lot of kids, I fell under the spell of a superhero when I was small and still wondrously unaware of any border treaties between my imagination and day-to-day reality. I got my own cape and set about readying myself to someday become part of the fantastical realm where he reigned supreme. No plans to run away or anything drastic like that—I'd just commute, which wouldn't be a problem since flying was one of my hero's talents. Meanwhile, I read everything I could about him, glued myself to the television whenever he came on, and pored over photographs of all the unique things he was continually creating to enhance

Umm, I got shortchanged worse in the cloning dept. Michael Jordan and I share way more in common!

his special powers. I studied his every move and even began to mimic his mannerisms like some kind of oversized featherless parrot. I didn't just admire him; I wanted to *be* him. Or at least a reasonable facsimile. I love Drew and all, but there had been a serious malfunction in the cosmic copy machine: I was meant to be David Copperfield's clone.

Thirty-two years after Copperfield first captivated me, I'm still a fan.

And while I did fulfill my dream of becoming an entertainer, there's a part of me that will always wish I became famous wielding a wand instead of a sledgehammer. Destiny's little sleight of hand, I guess. Still, the career I'm thrilled to have and the one I thought I'd have are intertwined in curious and surprising ways.

Magic became my "thing" at age 7, and I outgrew toy-aisle magic kits in no time. I was still in grade school when I began performing for an audience after Drew and I were hired as clowns for Parks and Rec. I would entertain kids at birthday parties with tricks like turning two lengths of rope into one without the benefit of knots, glue sticks, or used chewing gum. My biggest hit was a G-rated routine starring a pair of red sponge rabbits I called Mr. and Mrs. Bunny, who would magically reproduce twenty tiny baby sponge bunnies inside my volunteer's closed hand. Let Mommy and Daddy explain *that* when the party is over.

The constant honing of my craft on the home front didn't always draw the same appreciative response I got with sponge bunnies at birthday parties. I had a habit of cutting up my parents' newspapers every day—sometimes before they were done reading them—so I would have "ribbons" I could practice bonding together with a wave of my hand. I left a trail of shredded newspaper all over the place; it looked like a mini-tornado had touched down in a gerbil habitat. My mother likewise knew who to blame if her silk scarves, linen napkins, or company tablecloth went missing; her suspicions would be confirmed when I unveiled my newest routine at my weekly Friday night show for the family.

Drew turned out to be the ideal chump to practice on because, on occasion, he could be as gullible as I was crafty, falling for the same trick again and again. My favorite was to flip a coin to see who got stuck mowing the lawn (and we're talking acres here). Drew didn't figure out I was using a double-headed nickel for over a year. What a fool, trusting me! I could also cut cards in a way that—what astonishing luck!!!—favored me nearly every time. You'd think he would catch on and perhaps shuffle and deal on his own, but . . . no. (As long as you throw a few and let them win now and then, the chronically clueless won't start to suspect your deck is loaded.)

My self-education in the illusionary arts predated YouTube, and I relied heavily on the classic eight-volume *Tarbell Lessons in Magic* and its 3,000-plus illustrations to guide me from beginner to master, while also befriending local performers like David Wilson and Shawn Farquhar, who served as role models and sounding boards. Shawn was the magician's magician, having won every major award in magic, yet he still made time to mentor a skinny little kid with big dreams, and we've since become friends.

Maybe I enjoyed spending that time in the beautiful outdoors!

I joined the Vancouver Magic Circle and the International Brotherhood of Magicians around eighth grade and religiously attended the Magic Circle's monthly meetings, where magicians would spend a couple of hours swapping stories, holding mini-competitions, and performing for each other. Dad would drive me the 40 minutes each way and wait patiently in the car. He was my biggest fan when it came to magic. He would help me come up with ideas or gather materials to build my own illusions at home, and even began asking my advice on his own projects around the farm after I became adept at carpentry and metalworking.

Once a month, Drew and I would go downtown with Mom to help do some filing at the law office where she worked. It was good pay. Good pay for buying magic supplies. Every penny I earned there did its own vanishing act when I discovered there was a fabulous Diagon Alley–esque place called Jacko's Magic only five or six blocks from the law office. I would sneak off for extended lunch hours to pull books off the store shelves to thumb through, learn something, then put them back. The owner, Jacko, never kicked me out. He saw the passion I had and only wanted to foster it. Jacko displayed all the different effects in a long glass case. I would peer through the glass to study the coins, handcuffs, trick decks, cups and balls, and things that still to this day remain a mystery. If it was magic, it was in there, or on one of the twenty shelves that spanned all the way up to the 14-foot ceilings. I gladly spent my pay on beautiful silks for sleight of hand or playing cards with an extra-smooth finish so I could dabble in fancy flourishes.

I was around 12 when I finally got to see David Copperfield on tour. My parents bought tickets for me and a friend for his appearance at the Queen Elizabeth Theatre in Vancouver. As I settled into my

Jonathan

Drew

MISDIRECTION COMES
IN MANY FORMS.
SMOKE, MIRRORS, AND
SOME THINGS YOU CAN
NEVER UNSEE.
-Jonathan

sixth-row seat, I could already feel the anticipation buzzing through the audience like a electrical current.

Then the theater went dark, and billows of smoke swirled onstage like ground fog as music began to swell. An elegant, empty elevator appeared high above the stage and began its slow descent. I instantly recognized Copperfield's dazzling Heaven on the Seventh Floor illusion, and even though I knew what was coming next, I felt my heart race as the silhouette of a man slowly began to take mystical shape inside the elevator, floor by floor, as it lowered to the stage to the bone-chilling beauty of Phil Collins's song "Find a Way to My Heart." The door opened and there stood Copperfield, confident as could be because he knew: It was awesome. He hopped down to thunderous applause.

I spent the next couple of hours in a state of rapture.

When he asked for volunteers from the audience for certain tricks, I somehow managed not to squirm and make monkey noises like a spazzed-out second-grader trying to the get the teacher's attention with the answer. I sent him telepathic commands instead: *Choose me, choose me, choose me!!!* He looked right in my direction *YES, YES, ME!!!* then beckoned someone two rows down. *Oh, c'mon. You've got to be kidding!*

In my head, I started breaking apart his illusions to figure out how each worked, but the magic of Copperfield was about much more than the technicalities. I was drawn in by the showmanship, the music, the lighting, and especially the stories Copperfield told to build up his illusions. Magic wasn't something he performed; it was something he embodied. His passion breathed fire and life into the art. I felt trans-

More like tele-pathetic. LOL

Let's see: Play basketball with the guys or get locked inside a trunk alone, wearing a sparkly bodysuit? I've had tougher choices.

ported, still exhilarated and almost giddy from the wild ride when I left the theater and spotted people lining up around the side of the theater, screaming the star's name. Figuring it had to be the stage door, I threaded my way between all the elbows to a prime spot as Copperfield greeted fans on the way to his limo. When he approached my cluster of admirers to say hello, I managed to blurt out an introduction of sorts.

"I'm a magician, too!" I said. "I want to do what you do."

"It takes a lot of work," Copperfield replied with a warm smile.

My superhero had just spoken to me. I nodded.

It was settled, then. I'd do whatever it took.

By high school, I had the skills, custom illusions, and props to book gigs at small venues or clubs and even hired a few professional dancers to join me onstage. All efforts to recruit Drew as my assistant failed. It was a clear violation of the stunt-double-for-life clause in fine print on our birth certificates, but I let it slide.

At 16, I won 3rd Best Stage Performer in the Pacific Coast Association of Magicians magic competition. That's right: I was officially an Olympian of magic. Well, in my head, at least. I had also gained some local recognition with appearances on morning talk shows. I grew my hair out and started wearing a puffy leather bomber jacket and fitted black jeans like David Copperfield.

We once heard him say, "Do you know who I am?" to the bouncer turning us away from some dive. That must have been some other pleather pant-sporting conjurer.

I did think my alternate persona needed a flashier name, though. As I started performing more and more, I started imagining the sound of an announcer's voice, bringing me to the stage. "THE MAGIC OF JOHN SCOTT" fell flat. Even "Jonathan Scott" didn't seem to have the right ring to it, but I liked how "Jonathan" sounded. I remember sitting in the living room with Dad when we were bacheloring it in Alberta, building the ranch house. We'd been tossing ideas for a stage name back and forth, but nothing really grabbed us. Then Dad's face lit up. "I've got it!" he practically shouted. "You're Scottish and proud of it. Go with . . ." He drew out the announcement, waiting for a drum roll, knowing the suspense was killing me—and enjoying every second.

". . . JONATHAN THE LIONHEARTED!"

There was silence as I tried not to show the whole-body cringe on my face. Of all the amazing ideas my dad had come up with to date, this was not one of them. I mean, it would be a cool name if I were a knight, but missed the mark for a magician. I hurried past the awkwardness by explaining to Dad that I might have uncovered a secret tie among some of the greatest magicians of all time: They all seemed to have an element or color in their names. David COPPERfield. Harry BLACKstone, and even Harry BLACKstone Jr. What about . . . Silver? Nobody was using Silver. Jonathan Silver? "THE MAGIC OF JONATHAN SILVER." Holy smokes—that sounded amazing. It sounded like one of those names that you KNOW must belong to a famous person. With dad's hesitant approval (after all, it was no Lionhearted), it was official. That was the first day of the rest of my magic life.

I worked with a local artist in High River to come up with a caricature of me to put on business cards that offered the services of

Jonathan Silver, International Illusionist, for TV, film, and corporate events. No need for it to mention that I was in the tenth grade.

Everybody just started calling me Jonathan, onstage and off, and I eventually had my name legally changed as an adult from John Ian Scott to Jonathan Silver Scott. I didn't change my last name because, Lionhearted or not, I am proud of my Scottish heritage. Plus it would be strange for identical twin brothers to have different surnames. (And, frankly, I thought my dad would disown me if I did.)

In my late teens, I got approached about auditioning for a TV movie where they needed a magician to be the hands of the lead character. My agent asked me if I could roll a coin across my knuckles the way gamblers do. "Yeah, of course," I answered nonchalantly, making it sound like it was some nervous tic I couldn't stop doing even if I tried. Fact was, I had never rolled a coin across my knuckles in my life. It takes a ridiculous amount of coordination and concentration, not to mention tons of practice. There should be finger gyms or workout videos. I thought I had perfectly nimble magician hands, but my fingers had not been trained by Cirque du Soleil. My fingers were confused.

They say if you want to become expert at anything, you have to do it 10,000 times. Walking a quarter down my knuckles must have taken 100,000 tries. I started doing it everywhere to squeeze in the practice where I could. In the car, at dinner, in bed. It took about thirty hours of solid practice over several days before I finally nailed it. I went to the audition, performed the trick without a hitch, and never heard from them again. Since I knew my quarter-roll was spot on, I was left to wonder why my hands didn't get a callback. Were my thumbs stubby?

I really preferred creating tricks of my own, anyway. Most magic

Wow, I've heard of a face for radio, but not even hands for TV?

The Magic of
Jonathan Silver
International Illusionist
TV • Film • Corporate Events
652-7557

International illusionist Jonathan Silver expects to take the breath away from High River residents during his performance at the Highwood Memorial Centre on July 18.

● ENTERTAINMENT

Illusionist to wow High River

tammy McBRIDE
TIMES REPORTER

Jonathan Silver has a few tricks up his sleeves for High River residents.

The 20-year-old international illusionist plans to wow more than 450 people with magic beyond the impossible on July 18 at the Highwood Memorial Centre.

With 11 years of professional experience, the young illusionist is famous for his amazing illusions, dance and dare-devil stunts.

The High River resident's career began as a young boy with card tricks at birthday parties. He formed his first company, Top Hat Productions, at age 11.

"A lot of people think nothing can go wrong," Silver said, adding the audience usually doesn't know if a mistake is made. But Silver and his crew do.

Being a magician isn't always magic.

Silver has induced two injuries during his years of performing. A member of the audience was required to cut a rope in a rope trick and cut the end of his finger off instead.

During a rehearsal stunt in which Silver was required to hang upside down over three-foot-long spikes while trying to free himself from a straight jacket and suddenly appear in the audience, he fell, pierc-

Electrifying illusions

Jonathan Silver brings his exciting show to the Memorial Centre on July 18

page **14**

DAVID ERFIELD

Experience
The Magic Of
Jonathan Silver
International Illusionist

ONE Performance Only!

July 18
High River
Memorial Centre
8 p.m.
Tickets only
$10/Person!

A Spectacular Evening of Grand Illusion
For Advance Tickets Call Custom Design 652-1696
Or The High River Times 652-2034

Tickets Also Available At The Door

builders and inventors aren't performers, but I liked being able to design and build exactly what I wanted, tailored to my specific vision. I would even dream of performing an illusion and, the second I woke up, begin drawing it. Nothing was more gratifying than starting with the glimmer of an idea and coaxing it to life, from sketches on a piece of paper to months of rough drafting, meticulous measuring, sawing, welding, and adjusting until that moment when I was actually using my new effect onstage.

When I was helping my dad build our big ranch house in Alberta, he suggested we build a three-car garage with a vaulted ceiling so I could practice my illusions. I knew it was a ploy to get me to come home for weekends from the University of Calgary, and I was totally cool with that. Free food, laundry, AND a big space of my own? What's not to love? Whenever I went down to the ranch, I'd head straight for the garage, where I would get so lost in my work, I didn't even notice night falling or hear the winter winds howling outside. Magic consumed me. I ended up expanding my operation to the barn for manufacturing and kept the garage strictly for practice, rehearsing in front of big mirrors salvaged from a department store that closed.

Once I had worked out all the kinks with an illusion, I would deem it officially ready to perform. The feeling of using one of my illusions onstage was equal parts thrilling and terrifying. Thrilling to see a vision that had existed solely in my head become something real that others could enjoy. Terrifying because I'm an over-analyzer and there were SOOO many things that could go wrong. I typically worked out in advance a Plan A, B, C, D . . . all the way to Z. What if a caster breaks off mid-performance? *You need to ensure the prop doesn't tip over.* What if a door jams halfway through? *You need to make certain it's a break-away.*

What if a lion escapes and comes after me? *You need to remind yourself you don't have lions in your act.* Still, you never know! *Consider adding an emergency lion trap door.* In the end, I overbuilt the illusions to the point where they'd rarely break down. But MAN, were they heavy.

Even when it's DIY, large illusions like mine didn't come cheap. Drew and I had launched our first house-flipping venture soon after we got to U Calgary, though, and we were off to a strong start. The profits I didn't funnel directly back into real estate I'd invest into developing and building enough illusions to someday have my own touring show. At the same time, my years of immersion in magic fed my success with flipping: I loved the challenge of figuring out how to make something work, and how to dream up something beautiful and bring it to life.

Building the illusions was only half the challenge, though: These were massive pieces—some 10 feet tall and hundreds of pounds—that couldn't be hauled around in the bed of a pickup truck. I saved enough money to have a big trailer built with all the bells and whistles to safely haul all my props and gear. But I needed to build more of a name for myself before I could count on filling the seats for a multi-city tour.

I decided to give Vancouver another try—the city offered a lot more opportunities for aspiring entertainers, and we had just finished our latest flip. I left most of my props behind in storage in Alberta, along with some old illusions I planned to sell. Some I'd made, and others I'd bought. If I did book a gig, I would simply ship what I needed to Vancouver. Otherwise, I had enough magical supplies with me to cover any smaller performances. But my touring dream was still very much alive, and I managed to line up meetings with various touring companies and agents to discuss the possibilities. I could tell their wheels

were turning and they were interested in working with me. One of the secret superpowers I do possess is the ability to sell myself when meeting people face to face. As always, I kept inventing new illusions in my head. They could take months or even years to realize. Some, like my scheme to vanish the Eiffel Tower in broad daylight, were wonderful puzzles that I enjoyed working on for years.

Out of the blue one morning, I got a call from one of the touring companies I had met, and they wanted to work out a deal with me. If I had my show, ready to go and fully self-contained, they were willing to put together a tour. I was beside myself and absolutely wanted to make it happen. The problem was, I may have "oversold" how ready my show was: I didn't quite have enough illusions to do a full show. But much like the knuckle coin-roll incident from years earlier, it wasn't anything a little extra effort couldn't fix. I just needed to free up some cash so I could build the final couple of illusions I needed to complete my new show. Jonathan Silver was going on the road!

I went into overdrive thinking of ways to complete the show and about how incredible it would be. I had pitched the idea of a grand illusion show that would fuse magic with iconic movies and their famous scores. For example, I would wheel out a 15-foot translucent box on stage, which would start rotating as I was talking to the audience and demonstrating that it was empty before I closed its panels one at a time. *Jurassic Park*'s famous score would boom from the sound system, with smoke pouring out of the box as the music reached a crescendo, when the shadow of a giant T. Rex would appear inside the box and let out a mighty roar. The box would then explode open and expose a regular-size person in a dinosaur costume. The dino would hop out and pull off its mask, revealing yours truly, of course.

My dream seemed so close, and the images of how cool the show would be were vivid in my mind. The ideas were there, and I knew I could do the magic, but I still needed more props and illusions for this once-in-a-lifetime moment. I couldn't very well stand up there and do card tricks instead. I didn't panic, though. I loved problem-solving and had discovered in life that there is ALWAYS a solution.

Late that summer, I got a call from a stranger who introduced himself as a friend of one of my good friends. The caller was an escape artist who was expanding and getting into magic. He'd heard I had some props for sale and was very much interested in buying a few. I tried to get hold of our mutual friend to make sure this guy was legit, but every attempt failed. He was out of the country, and cell phones were just not commonplace at that time. Everything in my conversations with the escape artist seemed to check out, though. He had all the right answers and it really would be helpful to sell off these old props, so I agreed to fly to Calgary and show him the old pieces I had in storage.

The escape artist turned up with a woman and small child in tow. He seemed sincere enough, and how sketchy could he be with a cute tot right there in his wife's arms? He wanted to buy the entire lot of props I was selling and suggested we draft a payment plan. I felt leery of letting him take possession of anything before it was paid off, but he started talking about how this was his dream and how hard he'd worked to get this upcoming gig.

"What if you damage something?" I asked.

He assured me he would bear all responsibility. These props were vital to him, he added. In fact, he had another much bigger show he could book if there was a way he could use some of the props I wasn't planning to sell, too. If he could just borrow those until after his big show, he'd be able to pay off the full balance due on the props he was buying from me. Against my better judgment, I decided to give him a break. He was part of the magic brotherhood, not to mention a friend of my friend.

He seemed excited and grateful as he went off to make arrangements to come back with a truck and I headed back to Vancouver. He missed the first payment, then the next. I would call and ask for my money, but he would offer a bunch of excuses: His big show had been canceled; he just needed to do a few smaller ones, instead; the money was coming. I threatened to sue. Then he switched tactics: He claimed the props were all falling apart and unusable; he was going to countersue me for fraud.

Now I was in a dire situation. I had even fewer props than before, no money to build new illusions, and on top of all that, now I needed to get a lawyer. He had essentially cleaned me out, and ruined any chance I had to do a tour. In looking out for somebody else's dreams, I had inadvertently crushed my own.

Monetarily, the loss was in the neighborhood of $80,000. But that didn't even begin to account for the time, labor, and love that had gone into building the illusions. All those late nights drafting ideas, building in the barn, and choreographing routines were essentially now for nothing. A lifelong dream up in smoke.

I was 20 years old and had worked nonstop since I was 7 to earn the money I needed to pursue my passion, and now all I had were the small effects I'd brought to Vancouver and the few pieces the escape artist didn't take—that was barely enough to perform in intimate club venues, never mind a big theater. I was devastated.

It turned out that the mutual friend whose name the con artist dropped had never referred him, and in fact considered him shady enough that he would have warned me away. He was a fringe player on the magic scene. The thief changed phone numbers and names the way other people change socks. I wasn't the first— nor would I be the last person he ripped off. I managed to follow the trail of his various identities to eventually ferret out his real name and track him down.

In the end, every effort to hold him accountable in court just met with more evasion, lies, stalling tactics, or brick walls. I was finally awarded a judgment, but the court didn't understand what illusions were, so it only covered the cost of materials, which fell far short of covering the loss. And there was no way to recover my property, either: Turns out, the guy had sold my illusions as soon as he got his hands on them.

I quickly learned that a judgment was only as valuable as your ability to collect on it. The con artist had no property in his name to put a lien against. In fact, all of his assets were in his children's names so I couldn't touch them. I remember thinking how successful someone who was that smart could be if he put his effort toward something legitimate instead.

For the first time ever, I started having anxiety attacks. *How on earth did I get myself here?* I had invested every dime I had into my show. I had leased a truck, racked up my credit cards, and even taken out a loan to build a custom trailer. I was struggling. I had been so focused on putting my show together that I didn't realize the risk I was opening myself up to. I knew it would take years to recover what I had lost. I was depressed and destitute.

Not long after turning down the touring offer, I filed for bankruptcy.

If there's one thing I knew would always cheer Jonathan up, it was talking about magic.

I was too stubborn, proud, and independent to tell my parents how badly I'd screwed up, what a big mistake I'd made. During the process of the bankruptcy, all I was doing was servicing the debt I had on my missing props, my big trailer, and the white pickup truck I'd purchased to pull it. I had nothing to perform big theater shows with and wouldn't be able to dig myself out of the hole on my earnings from the "real" job I picked up as food/beverage supervisor at a local movie megaplex.

Drew knew how defeated I felt and went out of his way to try and lift my spirits by finding fun, creative things to do. Or by taping magic specials and sending them to me with ideas for new illusions. He had also started working as a flight attendant for an airline called WestJet and thought he could get me hired, too. He said the corporate culture was amazing, the travel benefits were insane, and the schedule was so light that we could still pursue other things. I applied immediately and was called in for an interview. The first question caught me off guard.

"What's a bizarre, unique talent you have?"

"Magic," I answered. The two women interviewing me lit up. They were both big fans of magic and wanted to know more. I performed a really simple vanish with their business cards, and they hired me on the spot.

I fit right into the company's fun, energetic culture. After all the stress I'd been under, it felt great to be surrounded by passionate, enthusiastic people who enjoyed what they were doing and cared about their jobs.

Up to this point, both Drew and I had always considered real estate a little something on the side to make some extra money. We had only been doing one property at a time and definitely taking our time with them. With the flexibility of our schedules at WestJet, I saw real estate as an opportunity to get us on more stable ground. My goal was still to get back to magic, but for now, my biggest reveals would be the beat-up shacks we transformed into beautiful, livable spaces. I guess it was still a form of magic, just less smoke and more framed mirrors.

First one year passed without me doing much magic, and then another slipped by, and another. Life was good, business was great, and I couldn't say I was unhappy. Just incomplete. We became the Property Brothers, and every now and then, I would slip a little magic into a show, like making a piece of fruit disappear for the homeowner's child or making a baby bunny appear out of thin air to be a friend for the pet angora rabbit that belonged to a client on *Buying and Selling*.

When we did *Brother vs. Brother* in Las Vegas one season, I shamelessly pitched that we make the reward for one challenge a tour of David Copperfield's secret warehouse full of priceless magic memorabilia and illusions. It is not open to the public and was something I had always wanted to do. There was no way Drew was going to win this one. I worked my butt off and claimed the reward.

I'd met David many times since moving to Vegas. We have mutual friends in the magic community, and I'd taken in his show several times. Sitting in his theater as a grown-up, I was every bit as awestruck as I'd been at age 12, when I told him I wanted to do what he did someday.

If you could make unrealistic clients disappear and more buyers with big cash offers appear, then I'd really respect your craft!

Copperfield's International Museum and Library of Conjuring Arts holds the largest collection of magic artifacts on earth, with more than 80,000 pieces that he has collected and preserved. On top of that, he has 15,000 antiquarian books on magic, dating all the way back to the 16th century. There's also an entire room devoted to the great Harry Houdini's personal treasures, from his first magic wand to his infamous Water Torture Cell.

In true Copperfield style, everything in the collection is meticulously positioned to tell a visual story and displayed like something straight out of a movie scene. Copperfield knows: Magic is about connection. There's an intimacy to suspending disbelief and inhabiting that childlike sense of wonder where what you see defies all laws of physics and all logic of reality.

David expressed to me his passion for fostering the art of magic and educating younger generations about how important the history of magic is. Not just to magicians, but to all of us. Magic has influenced the arts, cinema, literature, and in some obscure way, almost every facet of our modern world. The more stories he would tell me, the more I wanted to hear.

Copperfield is such a quintessential performer both on and off stage. He had even set booby traps for me, taking hilariously juvenile pleasure at every prank that nearly sent me into cardiac arrest as he guided me through the warehouse.

As we ventured deeper into the labyrinth to the far-reaching corner where Copperfield keeps his own illusions, that feeling of anticipation and awe I had as a little boy seeing his TV specials came flooding back.

Karma at last. I hope there were fruit flies.
Magician's code. I can neither confirm nor deny.

David had actually coordinated with Drew to find out which of his illusions were my favorites, and he had put them out on full display. Nothing could have been more perfect and as I stepped up onto his Heaven on the Seventh Floor illusion . . . I felt like I was stepping up in front of a packed auditorium. David hadn't performed this illusion in years, and after I wrapped up my own little daydream, I mentioned how cool it was knowing that I'm the only person who's graced this prop since he performed it masterfully so many years before.

"Actually, Taylor Swift used it to appear at the ACMs a few years ago and did an amazing job," David corrected me. Hey, I was still impressed with myself: If I had to come in third, it couldn't be to two more accomplished entertainers.

For weeks after visiting David's museum, I kept pressing rewind in my mind to replay the tour. This was actually common for me whenever I had some kind of magic encounter. Even simply seeing a show. Often I still dream in illusions, then assemble them, piece by piece in my mind. Sometimes, I'll hear a song and it will inspire me, and a story takes flight. That's what happened when I heard the beautiful song "Any Other World" by Mika, with a haunting chorus line that reminded me of years past: *Say good-bye to the world you thought you lived in.*

The illusion I set to that music takes place in an old attic. There's dusty furniture tossed about, and an old piano with a dingy white cloth draped over half of it. I'm up in the attic reminiscing about a love no longer with me. I see a framed portrait of her on the piano, snatch it up, and spin to center stage with it clutched to my chest. I then hold it up, facing away from the audience, only to see a life-size version of it illuminate at the back of the stage. I rush to it as the music builds. I grab a cloth from the floor in front of the massive painting and raise it as high as I can. There's a flash, and when the cloth drops, the girl has vanished from the painting and is standing—alive—next to me. The whole stage comes to life as crooked furniture straightens itself, and a tipped-over vase stands upright, full of fresh flowers. Our joy fills the entire attic with life and energy. We dance around the stage and make our way to the piano, playing side by side, bumping shoulders, laughing and giggling like children. I step up onto the piano and pull her up to wrap in an embrace when the cloth around us shoots like a ghost back to the painting, where my love reappears in 2D. She is gone from me again and the hurt is just too much. The music swells, and I grab another sheet from the piano. I raise it high above my head and instantly with a loud bang, I vanish from atop the piano and appear across the stage inside the painting with her.

I've turned out the lights in my living room many times to pace out how I will do the illusion. I've mentally constructed everything I need, and know exactly what color flowers and what shape the vase will be. I know how many steps, how many seconds, between the piano and the painting.

My life is filled with a different kind of magic now, an abundance of it, really, and I'm happy and grateful. I still feel a bittersweet twinge whenever I see a great performance onstage—every light, every gesture, every prop, every step, every single note of music coming together with such exquisite perfection.

I never did say good-bye to that world I thought I would live in, or to Jonathan Silver, International Illusionist, because the truth is, they never really left me, after all.

You might want to keep your eye on the Eiffel Tower.

THE WORLD'S **COOLEST** COIN TRICK

FIG A   FIG B   FIG C

FIG D   FIG E   FIG F

Jonathan

The entire effect is sold in the performance. You show your audience a regular coin and proclaim it has no hidden trap doors or secret strings. You may also let the volunteer test the coin—because for some reason they think that proves you're not cheating them. Oh, how wrong they are.

Hold the coin between your middle finger and thumb and turn your hand upside down. (Fig A)

Extend your arm forward with your palm elevated, so it is not in the way of a clear path for the coin to enter your sleeve. (Fig B)

With very little practice you will be able to snap the coin directly up your sleeve, and with a fancy flourish of spirit fingers, wave both hands back and forth, showing the coin has in fact disappeared. (Fig C)

For a little misdirection, tell the volunteer the coin has appeared in their back pocket. Before they think you stuck your hand where you shouldn't have, lower your arm, and the coin will naturally fall back into your hand. (Fig D) Joke off how that would have got you smacked.

Then reach up and magically pull the coin from behind the volunteer's ear. (Fig E) Suggest they wash more, and take your bow. You are now a master coin manipulator.

WARNING: DO NOT PERFORM IN REGIONS
THAT MAY BURN WITCHES AT THE STAKE.

LIFE IS ALL ABOUT
PURSUING YOUR PASSIONS.
I JUST HAPPEN TO HAVE
A LOT OF THEM.
-Drew

Comments by Jonathan

LIGHTS, CAMERA, ACTION!

I was home for the holidays at the family ranch in Alberta when the Ghost of Christmas Future came calling one night. Figuratively, not literally. No phantoms looming at the foot of the bed—just a nagging voice that sounded a lot like my own inside my head, insisting that it was time to take stock. Twenty-seven seemed a little young for the full-life evaluation, but clearly my subconscious was trying to send a message, and I needed to figure out what that was.

It was the end of 2005, the first year that Jonathan and I had committed to doing real estate full-time instead of using it as an ATM on the side. Once we decided to go

At least they distracted from the matching outfits we wore.

all-in, there was no holding back. Why wear water wings to do cannonballs off the high dive? We had thrown ourselves into the property game not merely to build a business, but a brand. People would recognize the Scott Brothers and know what we stood for—hard work, integrity, and always putting the customer first. (And, thanks to Jonathan's obsessive Photoshopping of our advertising material, teeth so white they looked radioactive.) We thought potential customers would take one look at us and think BOGO, two for the price of one, and in case they didn't get it, we underscored what a deal we were with our edgy slogan: "Get our team to work for you . . . you'll be glad you did." Clients were especially glad when we started throwing in a free moving truck, a bonus we had to discontinue because they thought we would be helping them physically pack and move their stuff, too. Umm . . . no. And you wouldn't want Jonathan to bring boxes, anyway, because he'd just make whatever you put inside turn into a rabbit. Or twenty. But our real stroke of genius (not) was when we shelled out a small fortune to have every theater in the city flash those ads with our glow-in-the-dark grins across every screen before every movie for an entire month. And it worked: The phone never stopped ringing. Teenagers would prank call us every time a movie let out. I'm assuming our faces came under heavy Sour Patch and Skittle fire, too. Was it worth it? No. After a month of running and a boatload of cash, we didn't close a single additional deal because of it. KHAN!

Needless to say, there was a big learning curve for us when it came to figuring out the whole self-promotion game.

But we're quick learners, and Scott Real Estate was doing well as our first all-in year came to a close. I mentally marked that as a "win" on the invisible scorecard and hurried to tally the rest of my accomplishments:

My car was paid off, and I had no debt. I had a college education, a real-estate license, and money in the bank. That all added up to success, right?

But am I happy? I wondered. This time the reply was swift and cut me to the bone.

Not really.

I didn't have to ask why: It had been 10 years since my last job as an actor. Acting was what I had planned to do with my life from the time I was a little kid, and Dad had used his old industry connections to get us on the set of *Look Who's Talking, Too.* Real estate was enjoyable, and had proven to be lucrative, but it was the profession that was supposed to support my Hollywood dream, not smother it with a pillow. How had a whole decade whipped by? *That's it,* I told myself. I made a decision, and dropped the bombshell on Jonathan:

"January first, I'm out."

I was going to pack up, move back to Vancouver, and give myself a year to pursue acting with the same energy and determination it takes to build a brand in any business. One last chance so I would at least have the satisfaction of knowing I tried my damnedest. I thought back to the advice Dad always gave us growing up, whenever anyone said we couldn't do something because we were too young, or inexperienced, or, most-maddening of all, because "It just doesn't work that way."

Was it something I said? Were you tired of me leaving my dishes in the sink?

*I usually just get it right the first time.
What can I say, I'm that good.*

"Go out and find five ways to do it, then," Dad would urge us.

It was like that old adage said, "If at first you don't succeed, try, try again"—except Dad's update made you "try, try, try, try, try" again—and he didn't mean the same way each time, either.

I'm the spreadsheet king, so once I hit Vancouver and had settled into Pedro's guest room, I started researching acting classes to sign up for, casting agents and network types to meet, events to attend or volunteer for—anything I could think of to get myself on the radar. I would even host casual get-togethers or dinners and invite directors, producers, and anybody else who got caught in my networking net. I knew the odds were stacked against me—and every other aspiring actor waiting tables or parking cars between cattle-call auditions—but I was going to treat the biggest gamble of my life like a poker tournament, not a spin of the roulette wheel. Save my emotion for the characters I hoped to play, and use my brain to stay in the game and get the chance. I was psyched to put my plan in motion.

It wasn't just acting that excited me: It was the entertainment industry as a whole. I wanted to get my hands in everything—writing, directing, producing, filmmaking, live shows. The math nerd side of me was curious to learn how the financing was put together for multi-million dollar features as well as artsy indie passion projects. The dreamer in me was already getting dressed for the premiere of a film written, directed, produced and starring . . . me.

*I can see it in flashing neon lights now:
Drew Scott IS "Delusional"!*

Getting an agent was my first priority. I knew that was going to take some salesmanship since I hadn't worked in so long and didn't have a resume full of major roles to begin with. I pitched myself to a friend's agent, who saw enough drive and talent to sign me but ended up semi-retiring a few months later and moving to an island off the coast of Vancouver. She said she could still represent me, but she was no longer in the heart of the action, and unless there was a major studio or two nobody knew about on her tiny island, I didn't see how that was going to work. On to Agent #2.

Agent #2 had just left a big agency to strike out on his own. He was trying to grow his roster of clients. He talked a good game, and I decided to give him a shot. What I didn't give him was the loan he promptly hit me up for to bail him out of financial trouble.

Fortunately, the third time was a charm, and my next agent not only was more reputable—and solvent—but came with a lot of bigger clients as well, which meant closer ties to top casting directors (which, in the trickle-down theory of actornomics, meant more potential auditions for me).

I wasn't kicking back and waiting for the scripts to arrive, though. And I wasn't holding out for a decent paycheck, either. Experience and exposure were what I needed most to establish my brand. Not that I would give Spielberg the brush-off if he wanted to discover me in the free-weights section at the gym. I had of course created a spreadsheet for my last-chance year in Vancouver, and networking was a top priority. Every day, I tried to take someone in the industry out to lunch to talk shop, gather intelligence, and make myself known. Mainly they were producers, directors, and working actors who were well connected in Hollywood North. I also registered for the actors' workshops that casting directors occasionally held. I was always willing to help people with small film projects because I hoped that someday I'd be the one asking for the same favor. Meanwhile, no-budget indie films were a good way to try and work my craft. I was hungry to immerse myself in a character, find out what made him tick, and explore his emotions. Maybe that sounds cliché, but when you love acting, becoming a character is like blending the paints on your palette in a way that renders the best color and texture on your canvas. That was my mindset when I was approached about one independent film project I'll never forget, try as I might. . . .

It sounded very cool and artistic. Visually, it was meant to be a stunning, quasi-*Romeo and Juliet*-style film. My only hesitation was that the character I was offered had a nude scene. I spoke with the director to ensure the film was going to be shot in a way that didn't seem amateurish or B-rated. Satisfied with the director's artistic vision, I agreed to take the part.

Oh, forgot to mention: It was a zombie film.

When you're a lovesick naked zombie, your craftwork is probably not the first thing the audience is going to notice. Especially not in this particular film, which in the end was as awful as they come. There wasn't anything artsy or creative about it. The storyline was lame. The cinematography was on a par with proud parents shooting their kid's recital with a video camera that requires them to hiss, "Is it on?" back and forth for an hour. My bare ass made its screen debut right in the middle of this terrible film. And no, I won't say the name of it. Ha!

Seriously? You wanted a sharper picture?

You were expecting Citizen Kane?

Knowing how competitive you are, I always thought Bloodsport 2 would be more up your alley.

Back in high school, when Jonathan and I were first putting together our acting resumes and portfolios, we drew up a list of all the special talents we thought would win casting directors right over in case our experience in school musicals and goofy home videos didn't do the trick. For starters, we were excellent at karate. And we had basically acted out all of Jean-Claude van Damme's movies and moves whenever and wherever we could, just in case anyone was considering a sequel to *Double Impact.*

Which brought us to another of the "skills" we listed: Twins. Not to boast, but that was something we had mastered over the years, and even though we were never mirror-image mimes, we were both veteran clowns. Jonathan listed his magic, and I threw in pretty much every sport that existed, including a few I'm sure even Webster was making up. Who knew Extreme Zorbing was a thing . . . but MAN, was I good at it ;-). There was singing, dancing, improv and, last but not least, we were excellent horseback riders. We were adolescent Renaissance men, box-office hits waiting to happen.

"Look at all we do! Who *wouldn't* hire us?" Jonathan concluded. A comedy featuring twin clown ninjas on horseback would be perfect, obviously, but we were open to anything.

Any delusions that the identical twin advantage would separate us from the crowd evaporated as soon as we walked into an audition and discovered four or five other matching pairs waiting to try out, too. It happened a lot. On my own in Vancouver, I still listed "twin" among

J - Guaranteed they couldn't ride a horse while singing Happy Trails in a German accent and juggling four tennis balls.

the dozen or so other Special Skills on my resume, which also mentioned rock climbing, cartoon voices, and college-level basketball. I was actually an avid athlete, and in the event I hadn't done whatever sport a director was looking for, I was pretty confident I could quickly learn enough to appear credible on-screen. I had second thoughts about that the time I landed a Coors Light commercial being shot over four days in Whistler, a world-renowned ski resort in British Columbia.

I was supposed to play a snowboarder, and there were three or four guys cast who were expert skiers. I admitted in the audition that I wasn't an expert, but I may have said I love snowboarding for fun. In reality, I had only gone once with Jonathan, and let's just say I posed no future threat to Shaun White. Everything was fine until they wanted to take us all up to film on a triple black diamond mountain, the toughest hill for expert skiers. I'm a thrill-seeker, but I'm not stupid about it: I knew I couldn't handle that, and I didn't want to kill myself. "He was pretending he could snowboard" was not how I wanted to be remembered. They shot footage to make it look like I was actually up on that hill with another guy wearing my outfit, but in reality, they only shot me down on the bunny hill. All of my shots were completed the first day, so I got to hang out at the chalet in the hot tub with the Silver Bullet girls for the next three. No regrets there.

Much as I longed to be in front of the cameras, I had to stay on point with the purpose of my year away from real estate, which was to know at the end of those twelve months that I had done everything I possibly could to realize my dream. This was about setting myself up for success by building the best foundation possible.

Luckily, I knew when to take emotion out of the equation. If I wasn't landing a part, I didn't take it as rejection or failure and sit

around licking my wounds. I continued taking classes and networking to improve my chances next time. I took private voice lessons and studied American dialect, as well. It was interesting to discover some of the subtle nuances that separate Canadian and American language. For example, I learned that Americans speak in clusters of words, whereas Canadians sort of ramble on in longer run-on sentences without taking a breath. There were also trick words like "about" and "house," which Canadians draw out to sound more like "aboot" and "hoose." The training was long and arduous but surprisingly helpful. As were the workshops on how to audition like a pro in the first place. A course in scene study at a top school called The Actor's Foundry made us drill so deep to explore emotion, it was like group therapy.

It was like strength training minus the pulled hamstrings. I found that the same coaching and visualization techniques I'd used back when I worked as a personal trainer were as effective creatively as they were physically. I also tapped into the wisdom of one of my personal heroes, Tony Robbins. I'd discovered his amazing motivational books while still in high school, and his message of positivity and creating your own destiny resonated with me even as a teen. I admired how Robbins had overcome a childhood scarred by abuse and abandonment, then went from janitor with no college education to "peak-performance life coach" with millions of followers and a fortune to match. I devoured every one of his bestsellers and bought all his VHS cassettes, then the DVDs.

I became a big believer in what Robbins calls incantations, which are like pep talks you give yourself, cranking affirmation up to full power. You don't just send yourself a quick mental valentine: You speak the words out loud, with body language and facial expressions that match the message and show your passion. In others words, you act out the part. Win-win for me. I rehearsed every day when I passed a certain house on my way to and from Pedro's place.

The house was an elegant Colonial with big pillars out front. Understated but impressive, I imagined it was home to a wealthy CEO or brilliant heart surgeon. It graced a manicured estate with green velvet lawn on either side of a long driveway that ended in a semicircle in front of the house. I spotted a fountain, too, and felt like I could hear the water splashing even though I was in my car parked on the street outside the arched wrought-iron gate and a 12-foot hedge. I stopped twice a day and delivered my incantation.

"I can have this house someday," I said. Forcefully, not wistfully. With the windows rolled up; no need to alarm the dog-walkers. "I deserve it. I am driven. I can accomplish anything I put my mind to. I will succeed." I invoked the same message when I was younger and pulled up alongside BMWs. It wasn't that I was trying to be a baller—I'm not flashy that way. And I wasn't planning some horror-movie scheme to drive the unsuspecting imaginary CEO/heart surgeon from the Colonial I coveted. I would get my own, and add a security system to discourage strangers from parking out front every day and weirding me out by having an animated conversation with an invisible passenger.

The incantations weren't to reassure myself that I was *capable* of achieving my goals, but to remind myself that every waking moment

Was lurking and lingering your method for attracting girls, too? Says the guy who pulled quarters from their ears. Voilà!

was an opportunity to do something about them. It's the difference between wanting someone to hold your hand or push you forward.

Keeping up the positive energy was more crucial than ever as my self-imposed deadline loomed. The year was nearly up, and I knew what it felt like when your all just wasn't enough. I'd been there once before.

I lived for basketball in high school and college, but I was a latecomer to the sport. I played for fun at lunchtime, but I didn't go out for the team until my senior year. I became a power forward and, at 6-foot-4, was considered respectably tall for a high school player. I tried to make up for the three years' experience I lacked over my teammates by showing up first for practice and leaving last. I was obsessed with basketball, and I was focused. I ended up MVP, though I still didn't have the seasoning most college-bound players did. When I graduated, I applied my athletic scholarship to UCalgary, intending to play my heart out for the team there and pursue a pro career. I knew I had the drive to realize my potential.

What I didn't have, as fate would have it, was the body.

The string of devastating injuries began with a horrible accident in early winter on a straight stretch of a two-lane highway in Calgary. Dad was driving, and I was riding shotgun. Mom was in the backseat. We were going about 50 mph when a teen driver up ahead hit a patch of ice while making a left turn onto the highway, and we crashed head-on. I looked over at Dad and saw that he was fine, then turned back to check Mom. All I could see was blood everywhere. I got out and wrenched her door open. Her face was split open, and I could see the bone beneath her nose, but she was conscious and coherent.

"I can't see anything at all," she said.

I went in the ambulance with her. Even with two black eyes and her face ripped open, she was cracking jokes to reassure me and, no doubt, not be a burden on the paramedics. They stitched her up at the hospital, and the next day, she went back to work even though she was so swollen and bruised, it looked like she'd been in a street fight and lost badly. "I'll just close my office door," she said. Doctors warned that there was a chance she could go blind because of the tiny bone fractures behind her eye socket; I can't help but think her positive attitude had something to do with her full recovery. I came out of the wreck with a knee injury, whiplash, and bunch of other bumps and bruises.

When I tried out for basketball at UCalgary, I didn't make the cut. Power forwards at the university level had a good four inches on me—and those were the smaller guys. The bigger ones went up to 6-foot-10. It just meant I was going to have to push myself harder. I decided to work overtime in the gym with weights and conditioning. I also invested in jump soles, highly unfashionable platform shoes from the 80s designed with the goal of improving your vertical leap . . . and preventing you from winning any runway competitions. After my first year at UCalgary, I moved back to Vancouver to play off-season with the University College of the Fraser Valley team for a while and just try to work through the pain.

My knee kept getting worse and worse, though, to the point where I couldn't straighten it. Some days, it would jut out at a 90-degree angle. I thought I was helping it by stretching, but it turned out that all I was doing was tearing the meniscus even more. I was limping around and felt so old, I half-expected to wake up some morning and find tufts of hair sprouting from my ears. *Which you would immediately mousse, no doubt.*

JONATHAN: We've never taken ourselves too seriously . . . I mean, how could we? Have you seen these faces?

DREW: Jonathan has been told many times that he has a face for radio. We have the same face, so I take offense!

I couldn't put off the inevitable any longer. The knee was only going to get worse without surgery, but the top sports surgeon had a waiting list of six months. Fortunately my coach at UCFV pulled some strings and got me on the surgeon's schedule within a week.

On the morning of the operation, when the doctor said they were ready to put me under, I bolted up.

"Absolutely not," I said. "I'm going to stay awake." I wanted to make sure the surgeon didn't take too much cartilage and leave me worse off down the line, which is what had happened to JD when he underwent the same procedure with a different doctor a couple of years earlier.

They gave me an epidural. The inside of my knee would show up on a monitor as the surgeon scraped away at the damaged meniscus like barnacles on a tiny shipwreck.

"No, no, I need the angle more toward me," I instructed as he began. "Sorry, but I need to see what you're doing. I have to make sure you're not taking more than you absolutely need to."

"Is this alright?" he'd ask as he zeroed in on another white mass. He had to find it annoying to be stage-managed by a college kid who thought a few kinesiology credits made him Hawkeye Pierce from *M*A*S*H*, but he was gracious enough not to show it. In hindsight, that was the first documentary I directed and starred in. I should have put *Drew's Knee* on my resume. Maybe add "Assistant Surgeon" under Special Skills while I was at it. Anyway, both the doctor and I came through the surgery in good shape.

At least until my ride home showed up.

Jonathan and Pedro. What was I thinking? The hospital should have kept me for brain surgery because clearly I needed it. Relying on the tender mercies of those two was just asking for it. They were proud graduates of the Marquis de Sade School of Nursing. When they came to fetch me, the epidural hadn't worn off, and I still had no feeling from the waist down. Jonathan and Pedro saw this as a wicked opportunity. On the short trek across the parking lot to the car, my legs were starting to get a little feeling back, but not much.

Jonathan and Pedro would pick me up, pretending to help, then fake distraction and leave me wobbling until my inevitable flop to the ground. They would repeat this shtick over and over as though experiencing it for the first time, every time. They thought their comedy act was gold, and if it weren't for my eventual recovery, they probably would have taken this show on the road.

The day after surgery, I was back in the gym taking shots at the basket. I knew I shouldn't try to jump, but my arms still worked. The UCFV tryouts were just around the corner. The coach didn't want me to risk it, though, and pulled the plug. "I know you're really trying," he apologized, "but you're not at 100 percent."

It took months of rigorous training and rehab to get myself back on the court. At the end of the school year, I went back to Calgary with the goal of trying out for the Mount Royal College team. I was determined to make it. However, within a week, I rolled an ankle on the court, strained the ligaments, and that was it.

Done.

Five years passed with me rarely touching a basketball. I was working as a flight attendant for WestJet when a passenger overheard me talking about basketball on a flight from Calgary to the tiny Alberta oil town of Grande Prairie. He turned out to be the head of the athletics department at a small college there.

"Come play for us," he urged me. He had a young, undisciplined team. He could use a more mature player. I couldn't believe I was being recruited at 25. It sounded too farfetched to be real, but on the other hand, it was so random that it had to be a sign, right? This could be it. My one truly last chance to play in-season college ball. Maybe it was too late to still picture myself playing alongside the pros I idolized, like Michael Jordan and Penny Hardaway, but if I didn't take this final shot, I knew I would regret it for the rest of my life.

I reported for a two-day tryout camp in Grande Prairie. We kept at it for eight hours a day. My heart was pounding out of my chest. By the end of the second day, I had busted a finger, been cracked in the nose, and hit in the eye by flying elbows out on the court. There were blisters the size of silver dollars on the bottoms of my feet. As beat up as I was, I felt alive. It was going to happen this time. I had lost out before and would not lose out again.

My winning moment came when we were playing a round of "kings court," which is basically one-on-one play where the coach could see how we matched up. I was on defense against a kid who was 6-foot-11. He had a cocky demeanor and was used to dominating on the court. But he was 18, and I could see through the tough exterior to the insecure immaturity inside. He drove to the hoop and then popped up for a short jump shot. I played the defensive dance like a pro and blocked him on the shot. In fact, I blocked him so hard I knocked him down to the ground. I then gained possession of the ball, circled around the three-point line and turned to the offensive. Before he could get up, I summoned all of my inner Air Jordan and took flight. Michael Jordan's signature dunk was from the foul line and I had emulated this for years. At 43 inches, my vertical leap was higher than that of many NBA players. I soared over the beached baller and dunked on top of him before he could even get up. This is the ultimate humiliation for another player. It was like me marking my territory on the court. Not five minutes after this, the coach offered me a spot on the team as power forward in the starting lineup.

I moved to Grande Prairie, enrolled in college, and convinced JD to get a transfer from the Calgary bank where he worked to their Grande Prairie branch. I bought a mobile home on five acres to live in and eventually flip.

After a few weeks, several truths started to sink in. I was in an oil town in the middle of nowhere, clinging on to an adolescent dream that wouldn't take me any farther. I was already considered to be in my golden years as far as a basketball career. On the other hand, I hadn't even scratched the surface of what I could accomplish in real estate or television. Most importantly, I realized I had left Jonathan struggling to run our business solo. I had made a big mistake. This wasn't propelling my life forward, creating my own destiny. It was going backwards, trying to rewrite what was already history. I finished fixing up the mobile home, sold it for a tidy profit, and headed back to the real estate business Jonathan and I were growing.

I couldn't regret making the move to Grande Prairie because it helped me refocus on what was most important. I had matured, and my new goals reflected that. When I made my decision to move to Vancouver to pursue my greatest passion, I appreciated the difference between fulfilling a fantasy and forging a future.

Yet here I was now at the exact same turning point I'd been at with basketball. Maybe my career in entertainment wasn't meant to be, either, but I still had a few months to give it one last Grande Prairie try.

Much as I enjoyed all the classes that jammed my Vancouver

calendar, I needed more hands-on experience, especially since I hadn't landed any notable roles yet. I was hungry to learn more about the logistics of creating a feature film or TV series. Jonathan and I had been making our own short films since high school, and I knew how to do an indie film for fun, guerrilla-style, but I wanted to get serious about it now. I approached a production coordinator I'd met to ask about interning with her. It was the major leagues. Big stars and multi-million dollar budgets. No naked zombies.

"You don't have to pay me," I offered. "I'll be your assistant and do whatever you need me to. Get coffee, run the copy machine, answer phones, whatever. I just want the education. It's a good deal for you, because I'm going to do the work of three students just out of film school." I was put on the payroll as a second assistant coordinator, pretty much the bottom of the food chain. They gave me a three-week project, and I kicked ass enough to be brought back as coordinator (the same position as the person who'd hired me in the first place). Each assignment thereafter boosted me up another level, until I was a unit producer, which meant I was pretty much running the production office.

Trying to soak up everything I could whenever I was on set, I kept spotting ways the production could be more cost-effective. Everyone was so wrapped up in the creative process, they were overlooking ways to make life easier on the business end. I wasn't in a position to tell them what to do, but that didn't mean I couldn't show them. My chance came during the filming of a movie called *Dancing Ninja*, starring David Hasselhoff as a mixed–martial arts fighter. When it came to shooting a big fight scene at the sports arena, the filmmakers realized they couldn't have an empty parking lot outside if there was supposed to be a giant match inside with crowds cheering. The lot should have been full of luxury tour buses and fancy sports cars, but there was no budget to rent them.

"Let me have that," I said. The gift of gab had served me well so far, and I went into super-salesman mode. I called a touring company and talked them into letting me have four buses. I lined up a small fleet of sexy new cars—a Ferrari, a Lamborghini, Corvettes, limousines. And we didn't have to pay a dime. That shoot day was a huge success, and the producers and director were blown away by what I had pulled off. Maybe I didn't get to live out my lifelong fantasy of playing a Marvel superhero onscreen that all-or-nothing year, but I felt like one that day.

I couldn't bask in the glory, though. There were more pressing issues on my mind.

I had managed to spend all my savings and run up all my credit cards over the course of that year. I spent about a hundred thousand dollars. My savings were completely gone, and I found myself lying awake one night in bed, my mind racing, unable to sleep for the first time in my life. I pictured myself at age 60, broke and living in a run-down apartment the size of a matchbox, contributing nothing to the world.

A Jim Cuddy single on the country charts kept playing inside my head, the chorus echoing for days. *"You could always pull me through . . ."* is how it went.

At first, I heard only a sad lament over something lost forever. But that line stayed with me, and the more I repeated it, the more I saw it as something else altogether: A message to my braver self.

An incantation.

I decided to regroup instead of retreat. I quickly got licensed in

Vancouver and went back to real estate. Jonathan had hired Geoff and Shirine Gordon, two brilliant Realtors, to fill the void when I left Alberta, and business had never been better. Expanding to British Columbia made sense. I could take on clients, still go on auditions, and keep working my new contacts in film and TV. Jonathan and I had both poured so much into realizing our respective dreams, but we were in no way satisfied or ready to settle. Destiny couldn't be done with us yet.

I dusted off my agent arsenal, eager get out there again and help people find their own dream to dwell in. I could use the same marketing materials Jonathan and I had developed. I made a mental note to have him tone down the high-beam smiles. Maybe the slogan wasn't so dumb, after all, though. *"Let our team work for you . . ."*

Am I ever glad I did.

BACK IN THE GAME, FIRST SALE IN VANCOUVER
AFTER TAKING A YEAR OFF OF REAL ESTATE
TO DO MORE ACTING.
—Drew

ROLE-PLAYING

Drew

Just to be clear, I have no intention of ever abandoning my hosting work with Jonathan. Too much fun. That said, I've become very good at balancing different passions, and I feel there are many roles out there calling my name. . . .

Superhero would be my dream screen role for sure. I loved Marvel and DC comics as a kid, so to play out my childhood fantasy of being superhuman would be amazing. I'd want one with plenty of white-knuckle stunts. Even better if I could swap out the tights for something cooler from my sock collection.

I've also always wanted to play a cowboy. That would be a great tribute to my parents and how we were raised on a ranch. Dad even wrote a feature Western script that I hope we can produce in the next five years. Any chance to delve into my Scottish history through a medieval character would be exciting, too. I could be a knight, king, or, as my closet full of shoes can attest, even a cobbler.

Like any actor, I'd love the opportunity to appear in a recurring role on a TV series, or be cast in a feature film alongside a powerhouse talent like Denzel Washington, Leonardo di Caprio, or Emma Stone.

One incredible role I was fortunate enough to play was in an indie film called *The Pulse*. I was a widower who fell asleep at the wheel and survived a terrible accident that killed his wife and only child. I dug deep

You just left yourself wide open for a Jester comment.

into the emotions of my conflicted character as he struggled to cope with the crushing guilt but open his heart to the healing love of a woman and her son who enter his life. Truly seeing the world through someone else's eyes, and experiencing aspects of depression, love, and remorse through him really took me to a deeper level of my craft.

As for the thanks-but-no-thanks list: I'm always looking to play roles that let me explore and experience the world through someone else's eyes. I'm not just looking to just play myself. Or even worse, Jonathan. Joke!

Oh, and not to hate on naked zombie lovers, but . . . been there, flashed that.

Jonathan

Drew is an adrenaline junkie and incredibly athletic. I know he would be in his element given a superhero role. You can get a taste of this in our Season Two promo for *Brother vs Brother*, which had us flying through the air on wires and doing all kinds of crazy things. The stunt team from *The Avengers* actually trained us. At the top of the Ironman drop, I got butterflies, but Drew wanted it higher and faster!

I could also see Drew in an intense *Law & Order*-type drama. He'd make a great renegade detective who relies on advanced math or sheer muscle to solve all his cases. On the opposite end of the spectrum, he's a total pushover when it comes to kids. He never gets tired of playing with them and they love his energy and goofiness. He'd be an awesome TV dad. Actually, that's a role I can't wait to see him play in real life!

What would I steer him away from? Accents. He's got the conviction of Meryl Streep but everything somehow comes out in this bizarre mash-up of Bengali and brogue.

LIFE CAN RUN
AWAY ON YOU IF
YOU DON'T TAKE
TIME TO SLOW
THINGS DOWN AND
EXPERIENCE LOVE.
-Jonathan

JONATHAN

Comments by Drew

ROMANCE

I t's no surprise that my most vivid childhood memory is from one of those long summer drives through the mountains. I was around 9. Our parents were in the front seat, holding hands across the console between them. Drew, JD, and I were all laughing our heads off about something in the back when I saw Mom lean over to kiss Dad. "I love you," I heard her tell him softly.

It wasn't like I hadn't heard them say that before—they were crazy for each other, and still are after 51 years of marriage. But that day in the car, a wave of pure contentment washed over me, and I wanted my life to always feel exactly how it did in that simple moment. *This is perfect*, I thought.

I felt that way again on my wedding day twenty years later.

I've never shared much about the impact divorce had on me, because why put something so sad out there? The pain ended up outlasting the marriage. The split isn't something I dwell on anymore, but for one too-long, too-dark period of my life, that's practically all I did. It shook me right to the core.

We met during a time in my life when I was dabbling in real estate on the side and trying to launch a career as a full-time professional illusionist. I honed my "mysterious" image by wearing billowy white shirts to set off that sun-burnished glow I got by regularly zapping myself with ultraviolet light in one of those tanning beds that toast you like a human panini. I was booking occasional gigs and performing in competitions on local talk shows, and apparently I was convinced that irradiation would make my magic even more magical. I was going for a shade of George Hamilton Mahogany in a semi-gloss, and the only other way to achieve that would be to sunbathe naked on the equator every day at noon. I was feeling particularly confident one day and started flirting with a casual acquaintance who had the kind of quirky humor I like. When she suggested I come along that night as she was meeting up with a group of friends, I happily joined the party. We discovered that we had a lot in common and began dating.

I was still pretty new at the whole relationship thing. My first girlfriend, Jen, had been kind but quiet, and preferred a cozy night at home to going out, which I could appreciate sometimes—but not all the time. I was more high-energy. I liked going out with friends, being social, and doing anything but sitting in one place to collect dust.

Jen and I never fought, but I kept wondering: *Is this what a relationship is?* I had no basis for comparison. After a few years, it was clear

I'll admit, Jonathan has always been a romantic through and through.

that we were stuck at "perfectly pleasant." But I wanted a cinematic love affair.

Anyway, we could have clung to our caring—if seemingly inert—relationship, but merely drifting along has never been enough for me. Difficult as it was, we needed to go our separate ways, accepting that we were simply different people who happened to be looking for different things. As my first girlfriend and the first person I uttered those three little words to, she'll always hold a dear place in my heart. I've never had an unkind word to say about Jen, and it always makes me smile even decades later when I hear she has checked in with my parents to say hello.

With this new relationship, there was no doubt that our lifestyles were compatible. There had been an easy, natural progression from hanging out to casually dating, then seriously dating. Within a year we were living together. I was 24 years old, but unlike a lot of guys that age, I wasn't a commitment-phobe. If anything, it was a relief to be off the market. I've had some embarrassing attempts at making contact with females of the species.

You've had some embarrassing attempts at even identifying your species.

If you mean that incident in Banff with the enraged bull elk chasing me through the woods, I was playing my bagpipes, not trying to seduce lady elk. Just a simple yet terrifying misunderstanding.

My uncanny ability to send the wrong signal goes back all the way to the third grade, which is the first time I thought I was falling in love.

There was this smart, beautiful girl in our class who was always drawing something, or doodling. Creativity, intelligence, good looks— she was a goddess, and I spent months trying to figure out a way to talk to her. Besides, of course, just going up to her and saying hi. That seemed far too lame for a woman of such mystery. Drew and I didn't grow up with sisters hanging around, and all our friends were other boys, so we had no practice when it came to socializing with girls. The artist was about to be my beta test.

But first, I had to overthink every possible scenario. How would I even get her attention? Pretend I needed to sharpen my pencil every twenty minutes so I could walk past her desk and pointedly ignore her? Throw spitwads? Offer to sell her some of our decorative hangers at a friends-and-family discount? And where should this staged encounter take place? Did she already have an artsy boyfriend? LOL. The longer I waited, the more scenarios of what could go wrong my imagination concocted. The school PA system, for example. What if it was on, and my attempt to talk to The Goddess was broadcast to every classroom, then replayed in the cafeteria at lunchtime? For that matter, did the school code of conduct include a formal rule against talking to girls? Could I get detention? What if she just started crying? I was always scripting and starring in my own mental disaster flicks when I was a kid, and the tendency still sometimes creeps back into my decision-making process today. It's exhausting.

Finally, one day after class, as the rest of the students poured out of the room, I noticed that The Goddess was still at her desk sketching

I always knew you'd use the twin thing to pin a crime on me.

something. She was so focused on her artwork that she didn't seem to notice that everyone had left except me. This was my chance. Fate was my wingman. If I didn't make my move now, maybe I would never have another shot.

With one fluid motion, I got up from my miniature desk with the chair attached (without knocking it over, thus averting Imaginary Catastrophic Scenario #1) and walked up behind her. Her perfect head was bowed, her silky black hair falling like an elegant curtain across her masterpiece in progress. I leaned over her also-perfect shoulder and only got out "Whatcha workin . . ." before a massive pool of drool fell from my mouth right onto her drawing. It all happened in slow motion. The drawing was ruined. The Goddess was grossed out. I was too humiliated to think straight and simply said, "I'm Drew." Followed by an exodus so swift I could have made it the finale vanishing act in my future grand illusion show.

It took me three years to work up enough courage again to show a girl I was interested.

This time, I was going to be direct and to the point. No more mincing around. Blame it on puberty: I was a man on a mission.

The target: Heather.

The objective: My first kiss.

Heather had long blond hair and freckles. She was as kind as she was cute. Best of all, we were friends already, and I made her laugh. Obviously we were meant to be together. Obvious to everyone but Heather's boyfriend, that is. Fortunately it wouldn't have to come to death-by-dodgeball if my plan worked. The boyfriend was one of the popular skater kids who seemed to date a different girl every semester. Nice enough, definitely cool, but not a romantic like yours truly. Not that I had anything to base my self-proclaimed Casanova status on, but I just knew I could be more.

One day, Heather and I were out sitting on the swings in the schoolyard during our lunch break. Her boyfriend was away on a family trip. We were talking about what was likely some critical plotline in our Real Housewives of the Fifth Grade social world when my brain relayed an urgent command to my lips: YOU MUST KISS HER!!

I blurted out an 11-year-old's version of a Shakespearean sonnet: "Heather, if you kiss me, I'll never bother you or talk to you ever again. I promise!"

I was staring straight forward because I couldn't make eye contact. There was silence, broken only by the rusty squeaks of the chains on our swings. Then that stopped, too. She was standing in front of me.

"How about I kiss you, and we still stay best friends?"

Only a girl with a heart of gold would have known that that was the perfect thing to say. Neither of us told Skater Boy, and I wasn't disappointed that our friendship never blossomed into more. I would always have that gift of a perfect first kiss.

In eighth grade, the awkwardness ante got upped yet gain when Drew and I met a pair of identical twins our age. Jackie and Jen were so alike, I don't think *they* were even sure who was who, and we honestly didn't have a clue. Contrary to popular belief, twins do not possess some freaky power that allows them to instantly tell other twins apart. Maybe dolphin twins can, but not human ones.

The four of us became fast friends despite the confusion. We'd have movie nights, play sports, and do just about everything together as twin-friends. I remember joking how we could never date because we'd need ID bracelets or tattoos to differentiate between us.

Jackie and Jen were pretty, athletic clones destined for instant popularity in high school, while we were the nerdy karate twins who could only hope that the goodwill we were banking in eighth grade would pay off in ninth with groupie seats at the Cool Table after their matching blond stars rose. Our odds improved considerably when the friendship segued into very low-key dating. "Very low-key" is beginner dating, so squeaky clean and G-rated, we could have qualified as gray-market Osmond brothers. "Advanced" dating was defined as hot-and-heavy, which implied that the couple in question had "gotten to third base," though no one, including the couple, was entirely clear where that was, much less what you were supposed to do upon arrival. Eighth grade was the Year of Wild Speculation. I, for one, was happy to play it safe with Jen and Jackie or Jackie and Jen, whoever they were. I still didn't trust school PA systems, and no way was I giving this one a chance to publicly broadcast my progress—or lack thereof—around the mystery bases.

In no time at all, the double-twin thing became more of a nuisance than a novelty, though, and waaaaay more complicated than any very-low-key-where's-first-base-again relationship should ever be. It was awkward enough to lean in for a kiss hello only to realize too late that this one was your brother's girl, and it should've been just a hug.

It's even worse to find that you've become a social experiment that everyone feels entitled to observe and discuss. Including your social

Me standing right there holding her hand should've been a clue. LOL

studies teacher. "You realize if you marry, your kids will all have the same DNA and look alike," he said, easily winning the How Much More Awkward Can This Possibly Get? challenge. Nothing can quash young love as horrifically as learning that your future children will be assembled from a communal pile of similar features like a Mr. Potato Head game. We were starting to feel like more of a gimmick than a romance, anyway, so the four of us beat a hasty retreat back to the safety of the friend zone. (Jackie and Jen did, in fact, advance to the cool crowd in high school, but they were still always nice to us. Twin code.)

I never dated in high school. I had girls who were friends, but never an actual girlfriend. Chrissy fell somewhere in the maddening middle. I'd been attracted to her for a long time, and we'd become close pals, but never a couple. Unlike swing-set Heather, Chrissy wasn't someone else's girlfriend, though, which gave me a sliver of hope. I finally made my move in senior year and asked Chrissy to go to prom with me. She laughed.

"No, that's not going to happen," she said. If this was her idea of letting someone down gently, she had a bright future in pro wrestling.

Chrissy? The girl I went with to prom?

You didn't "GO" with her.

Yeah, actually, I did. We went in the same car, and I gave her the corsage. You do the math. I also remember thinking how funny it was that Mr. Suave Magic Man got rejected.

Either I blacked it out of my memory, or you're messing with me. Prove it!

. . . I legit don't remember this. But I'm over it because I went with my best friend, Michelle. And we had the best PG-rated time ever.

Drew

Jonathan

Chrissy   Michelle

She had always been reserved, so the smackdown was even more stunning. I was really upset: How could someone be so rude, especially when they were supposed to be your friend? It turned out that she meant *no way did she think her strict parents would let it happen*, but that's not what my sensitive, inexperienced ears had heard.

By the time I met my ex, I had gained some recognition as an illusionist, and found I could tap into some of the self-confidence I had as a performer when I ventured into the dating world. If I spotted a woman I wanted to meet at a party or bar or some event, I didn't approach until I had thought of something funny to say. Comedy was always my icebreaker. Then, if she laughed and seemed interested, I would bring on the magic. Ask someone for a coin, then make it vanish and reappear in a beer bottle, and there's a good chance you'll grab her attention. There was an even better chance I could hold onto that attention for the night if I folded her paper cocktail napkin into an origami rose and made it levitate.

The woman I married was easy to be with from the start. She was sociable, and always up for fun, whether it was going out with a bunch of friends or just the two of us packing up to jet off somewhere together. When we first met, I was working in the emergency response department for WestJet. Getting to fly almost-for-free was the best job perk ever, and I took full advantage of it. We would take several big trips a year—island-hopping in the Caribbean, exploring some romantic city in Europe, or maybe chilling out on the beach in Mexico.

Even after I quit the airline to tend to my growing real-estate business full-time, we'd get away as much as we could, even if it was a quick weekend jaunt. Las Vegas was a favorite destination: We loved going to the shows, hitting the hottest new clubs and restaurants, and meeting up with my magician friends based there. I could easily picture myself living in Vegas someday, fulfilling that lifelong dream of following in the footsteps of the greats like David Copperfield. My girlfriend could envision relocating there, too. The sensory overload of the Strip's glitz and glamour was thrilling compared to Canada's quiet, natural beauty.

I've never been a big spender. I'm not a guy who needs fancy, expensive toys. I don't care to own enough clothes to open a department store. My ex had more discriminating taste, though, and I did like being able to indulge her. Okay, so maybe I did have a secret, shameful obsession with women's handbags and, since it wouldn't be prudent for me to carry them, maybe I did use my girlfriend as an excuse to keep buying them. She enjoyed getting more shoes and accessories to go with the designer bags, of course. What can I say? If we were headed for Hoarderville, I knew from years of flipping people's houses that there were worse routes for getting there. At least she didn't collect dryer lint or taxidermied squirrels or something.

Business was thriving, but I didn't have to be a self-proclaimed math genius like Drew to know that we were overspending, and it was starting to make me nervous. Cutting back on the travel seemed like the obvious solution. It wasn't just the expense that was causing stress: The fun getaways were so frequent they'd become the expected norm. Some couples went to the movies on the weekend; we went halfway across the country for dinner on Vancouver Island. It was a letdown if I couldn't pull away from the job to take off somewhere. My hours may not have been as structured as a nine-to-five boyfriend's would have been, but I only had to put in an average of five hours a day. I

But dryer lint smells so good!

told myself that my girlfriend wanting more time together just underscored how in love we were. After all, we never argued.

She wasn't shy about reminding me that the wedding date of her dreams was July 7, 2007. What could be luckier than 7/7/07? When she first mentioned it and I joked that 10/10/10 sounded good, too, she made it clear that this was no laughing matter. I got the message: That date was important to her.

Even though I felt like I was still discovering her, I didn't put up any real resistance to the deadline. Maybe I wasn't experiencing that overwhelming sense of *this is perfect* yet, but I was certain that what we had was a good, solid, healthy relationship. *Why are you taking your time?* I chided myself. *You're in love, why not?*

With the summer of 2007 looming, I decided it was time to propose and, since we both loved Vegas, I knew I wanted to pop the question there. I called the hotel to let them know I wanted to do something memorable. What were the possibilities? They suggested dinner at their restaurant and having the engagement ring hidden in the dessert. What if she choked on the diamond? That wasn't the kind of memorable I was going for. Besides, that proposal was so old, Eve probably would have found a solitaire in the apple if she'd taken a second bite. I didn't want generic . . . I wanted *epic*.

I came up with my own plan, and on a Wednesday afternoon, the plot was unexpectedly set in motion. "Hey, some friends are heading to Vegas for the weekend," my soon-to-be-fiancée told me. "Wanna go?" I smiled calmly and agreed, but it was panic in the streets inside my head. I had so many calls to make and so much to do if I was going to pull my plan together in 72 hours. Fortunately, I had already done a lot of the legwork and really just had to knock over the first domino.

When we got to Vegas, I created a plausible ruse to break away for a stealth meeting at Tiffany's. I had sent advance word of what I was looking for, so they had different stores around the country pull a selection of rings and send them by courier to Vegas for me to choose from. I had always loved the beauty and simplicity of the Tiffany's solitaire, and we both loved the film. So for me, this was the only way to go.

I love to plan special dates, so she was excited but not at all suspicious when I surprised her one evening with a champagne helicopter tour to see the city lights. What she didn't know was that I had planned my own little light show, too. As we swept over the neon fantasyland below us, I kept my eyes peeled for what lay ahead.

"What's that down there?" the pilot asked with fake curiosity as the helicopter flew out of the city and over the surrounding desert. She turned to look, then did a double take. "What the . . . ?" Projected in light across the desert floor was my proposal, spelled out in letters 40 feet tall:

MARRY ME

When she wheeled back around to look at me, I was as down on one knee as you can get in a helicopter, waiting to put the ring on her finger. (Her "Yes!" was a relief in more ways than one: I had kept the ring hidden in my sock for hours, which had proved to be incredibly uncomfortable.)

We exchanged vows on 7/7/07.

But the marriage was in ruins before our second anniversary.

When Canada's economy started wobbling in 2008, Drew and I were spared the devastating blow a lot of people in real estate suffered because we weren't over-leveraged and in fact were only upside-down on my marital home. We'd realized it was too risky to do any more flipping until the market stabilized. The Great Recession had hit the U.S. before it reached us, which meant our neighbors to the south were farther along in the recovery process. Bearing that in mind, we felt the time was right to expand Scott Real Estate, and Las Vegas was high on our list. Vegas had been ranked one of the world's fastest-growing economies in 2007. During that boom, the demand for housing was so great and the supply so limited that developers were actually selling lottery tickets to buyers clamoring just for the chance to even bid on a place. When the bubble burst, lots of new construction projects were left half-finished, and scores of existing homes went into foreclosure when owners couldn't make balloon payments on their mortgages. It was a good time to invest in fixer-uppers.

Drew was living in Vancouver, working on his acting career and paying the bills with his roster of real estate clients, so JD came along for the adventure when we moved to Vegas at the end of 2008. I was looking forward to the desert sun when I left Canada behind that December. It was just my luck to arrive in Las Vegas in time for a rare snowstorm that all but paralyzed the city. It dumped less than 4 inches just outside downtown, which saw no accumulation whatsoever. Still, the snowfall shattered a thirty-year record of less than 3 inches. I was dismayed but hardly discouraged: I'd accumulated more snow than that in a single boot back in Alberta. *Seriously?* Call me when you've got enough for a drift.

My visa allowed my wife to live and work anywhere she wanted in the States. We both had high hopes for this big move—for me, it was as much about magic as it was real estate. Vegas is paradise for anyone passionate about live entertainment. Even if I weren't performing full-time, the sheer number of venues, events, and potential opportunities to do magic was energizing. My wife, meanwhile, was offered a job as a poolside waitress/model at the "day club" of one of the big hotels, where the booze flows like water and the tips are high.

And things started going downhill from there.

Hotel-casinos in Vegas are obviously hyper-competitive, and the bars were prime feeder-chutes for the gaming tables. The pressure to create the hottest bar scene on the Strip was especially intense as the tourist-dependent town struggled to its feet after the crippling blow of the recession. The hostesses, bartenders, and servers would get off work from the day clubs, then be expected to go out partying together from rival bar to rival bar in an attempt to lure wide-eyed tourists to their employer's property. It was survival of the fittest, dirty with extra olives. The high-decibel buzz at a bar impossible to get into on a random Tuesday night could become the sound of crickets by the following week if they weren't playing their recruitment cards right. My wife was out every night, coming home later and later. She had a whole subset of friends now that I barely knew, and I was rarely invited to join them. "It's work," she would sigh wearily. Work seemed to be putting more and more distance between us.

Our first fight happened the day I discovered my wife had scrubbed me from her Facebook page, changing her relationship status from Married to blank. What had I done to be publicly disowned as her husband? Surprised and hurt, I confronted her.

"I don't want people at work or customers knowing about my private life," she explained. I'd been a server back in the day, too, and I knew full well that charm and connecting with your customers is what brings in the big gratuities. I didn't begrudge my wife that, but I couldn't pretend I liked the idea of trolls who checked her out later on FB getting the false impression that their hot cocktail waitress was single. "It's not a big deal," she tried to placate me.

"It should be important to you because it's important to me," I argued. This felt foreign to me. Fighting was just not something we did, but not emphasizing that had already cost me a treasured moment on our wedding day, and I wasn't going to swallow the hurt again. She would not agree to have bagpipers play at the ceremony in honor of my family's Scottish heritage. All the men in the wedding party did wear kilts, but the Scott clan still felt wounded by the bag-pipe ban, and I regretted not holding my ground about something so important to me. I guess that was a yellow traffic light that I blew right through.

We got past the Facebook fight, but it would be a lie to say there was a relationship rewind button that put us right back into our happy place. I couldn't remember a single night spent apart as husband and wife, so it felt strange to pack up for Canada without her when a pro-duction company came calling.

Some television producers had had their eyes on Drew for a TV hosting gig, and he had shown them a sizzle reel we had made for an audition a few years earlier, featuring a fun makeover of JD's place. Sizzle reels are basically montage videos on Red Bull, a quick taste of what the show's about, who will be in it, and where it's set. Discovering that Drew had a double who happened to be a contractor/designer gave Drew's producer pals an idea: Would the two of us be interested in testing for a show they had in the works called *My Dream Home?* The idea was to help desperate buyers get into the home of their dreams via a fixer-upper. That was exactly what we'd been doing for years, anyway, minus the TV audience. It was a no-brainer to tell the producers we'd be right over. Over being Toronto, that is.

The production team flew Drew and me up for a few days to shoot the *My Dream Home* sizzle reel. Even the excitement of gaining momentum on the professional front couldn't completely take my mind off the feeling that things were inexplicably faltering on the personal front. It felt like my wife and I were adrift on an open sea, unsure of whether the fluctuating tide was going to carry us away into the sunset or pull us straight under.

That first night I was away, I couldn't stop thinking about her. I texted her several times to see if she wanted to hop on a call before I headed to bed. After a couple of hours, she responded saying she was out with friends and would call me after. She was on Pacific time, and I was three hours later on the East Coast, so my inner clock was already struggling to tick. I drifted in and out of sleep, listening for her call in my isolated little hotel room. I was lonely. I missed my wife. When my six o'clock alarm woke me in the morning, I silenced it and checked my phone only to see that no call had come in. No text had been sent. My mind began to spin as I wondered if she had tenderly avoided calling so as not to wake me at such a late hour, or if she had never quite made it home at all. In Vegas, it's not inconceivable to party through breakfast. And lunch.

That uneasy feeling that something wasn't right reminded me of the time our elementary school decided it would be good for our individual development to assign Drew and me to different classrooms for second grade. The separation wasn't as bad as my tenth-grade solo crash-and-burn in High River years later, but we both felt vaguely anxious and out of sorts. The teachers and our parents agreed that our energy was just off and didn't try to split us up again.

A month flew by, and we were still waiting to hear whether *My Dream Home* would be picked up. I had promised myself not to get my hopes up, but I couldn't help it. This was a big opportunity and would be totally life changing. Those daydreams would often be abruptly shut down as reality snapped me back to the problems in my marriage. Things were getting worse, and we needed to fix it. Open, honest communication may get rough at times, but I'm a steadfast believer that it's the only way to go in any relationship you care about. I approached my wife, hoping to talk directly about the massive elephant in the room.

"You know I'm not thrilled about the Facebook thing," I began, "and it's no secret that things have been off with us." I plowed ahead, keeping my voice steady as I cracked open the door. "I think we really need to talk."

She agreed, and we began to discuss the highs and lows of our current situation.

I asked myself if I had somehow failed her as a husband. I had never been unfaithful. Or even disrespectful. I cherished this woman, and I wanted to spend my life with her, to love and be loved by her for the duration, whether our journey was full of adventure or adversity. I had been lucky enough to grow up inside a love story, and I didn't want to close the book on my own. I wanted to throw my last ounce of energy into fighting for our marriage, for her. We just couldn't seem to make the connection anymore. The distance between us grew wider, the silent nights colder.

There was a surge of hope when we agreed to marriage counseling, but that was short-lived, as she decided not to continue attending.

Sitting in the therapist's office alone sealed the fate of our marriage and brought me clarity about it. She moved out, and we filed for divorce.

There's a twelve-month waiting period before divorces are finalized in Alberta, where we were married. I was determined to keep things civil between us. When her mother came to town and said she wanted to see our two dogs, Gracie and Stewie, I got her free tickets to a Blue Man Group show and invited her over to the 5,500-square-foot house Drew and I had bought in foreclosure and planned to renovate someday.

The divorce dragged on for another hellacious year as our respective attorneys exchanged missives. There's no victory to such an inherently brutal process. I was in such a negative place, it was hard to even enjoy the ride as *Property Brothers* took off. Defeated, depressed, and alone again in a Toronto hotel room, I finally just called my ex directly one afternoon.

"How did we get to where we are?" I asked with genuine sorrow. "I don't get it. This isn't who we are. You can have two good people who just are not good together, and it's not a sin." I could hear her sadness on the other end of the line. We were able to talk the way we used to and signed our final papers the following day.

We were done.

Except I couldn't move on.

When I came out of my marriage, I was hurt, angry, and felt completely lost. I had mentally plotted out the rest of my days to include this woman . . . and now she was out of the picture completely. Being in a relationship, to me, meant knowing that no matter how bad your day was, there was one person who would always have your back, as

I could tell Jonathan was still hurting, which hurt me. I'd try to get him to go out with me, but he'd usually politely decline, saying he had to get home to Gracie and Stewie. The fun-loving, happy doppelganger I'd known my whole life was now a faded shadow of his vibrant former self. They say time heals all wounds, but they don't say how hard it is to watch the second hand tick on your loved ones. I made it my goal to remind Jonathan that we were all there for him.

you would have theirs. Maybe having a twin made me understand that kind of ride-or-die devotion early on. But my marriage had failed, and that left me questioning the loyalty in all of my relationships. Loyalty is something I always have, and always will, treasure deeply. I see it as a quality that reflects more than even love; it says something about character, too. Had we tried hard enough to fix what was broken? If we were truly loyal to each other, wouldn't we have tried harder? I was left with far more questions than answers and needed time to reflect on all of it.

I lost all desire to socialize and shied away from family and friends. I didn't want to risk getting hurt by anyone, lover or not. The only company I could enjoy was that of my unconditionally loving pooches, Stewie and Gracie. They never judged me, wanting nothing more than love in return and maybe the occasional treat. In them, I found solace.

I poured myself into the show, willed myself to put up a happy front for the cameras, then returned to my funk when we wrapped for the day. Sometimes an unknowing acquaintance might ask how my wife was, never realizing what pain their polite small talk would cause. I found comfort in routine and didn't miss going out to bars and social gatherings. In fact, I didn't even go out on a date for over six months.

It's one thing to face a personal tragedy. Another to face it alone in isolation from your friends and family. Filming in Toronto, I was in a city where I didn't know anybody. I was unsure of my way around, and I hadn't built up the courage to get back out there. With our filming schedule, Drew was only in town part of the week, so I didn't have him to lean on. But even when we were together, I never liked to talk about "it."

I realized that I had this great circle of friends—very caring, compassionate, kind people whose strength could pull me out of this sinkhole faster than I could climb out by myself. Many of them chose to fly out to Toronto to visit, which meant the world to me. Before I knew it, I was smiling and laughing again. It was a feeling I had missed deeply.

Once I ended my self-imposed exile from every female alive, everyone wanted to set me up. But I hate blind dates. I hate blind dates more than words can possibly convey. But I couldn't keep third-wheeling it on dates with Drew and Linda forever, no matter how generous they were about sharing the tub of buttered popcorn at the movies. I told my matchmaker pals that I was attracted to insightful women who had their own passions in life and were following them. They'd swear they knew the perfect person for me. I'd go on the blind date, and it would be terrible. Like, please let there be a citywide blackout before the salad comes so I can slip unnoticed into the dark night, terrible.

"What on earth made you EVER think that would be a match?"

I would demand of whichever female friend had missed the mark so wildly this time. Invariably, the guilty party would shrug and look perplexed.

"Well, you're both single," came the eye-roll worthy reply. That's like saying you're compatible because you're both right-handed.

My own brother even tried to pimp me out. We were booked to appear on Steve Harvey's talk show, but while we were sitting there yukking it up, this wall opened up on set and there sat three beautiful women. *Surprise!* It's the Dating Game! I had to interview the eligible bachelorettes and then choose one to go on an instant date with, which turned out to be lunch in the studio cafeteria. She was perfectly lovely, but it was painfully awkward.

I took charge of finding my own dates from then on. I had accepted that my ex-wife and I were simply not meant to be. There was no need for a hasty generalization of females or any lingering negativity. I was ready to trust women again, but I honestly didn't know if I would get in another serious relationship. I spent five years going out on some great dates as well as some disappointing ones. There were some sparks and a couple of wonderful women, but no show-stopping Fourth of July fireworks with cannons booming and the 1812 Overture playing in my head. I told myself I was okay with that.

Then, in September 2015, I was walking the red carpet at a charity event in Toronto when I saw this gorgeous, tall blonde standing at the other end in a group of people who seemed to be hanging on her every

I always assumed it was "Magic Man" playing in your head. How could you hear it over "Creep" playing in yours?

word. I had never seen her before and didn't know any of the people in her group, but I was intrigued.

At the end of the night, as I headed toward the exit, I spotted the mystery girl again, sitting at the back of the room at a table by herself. There was no time to stop and plan something witty to say, so I just stopped in front of her and blurted out the first thing that came to mind, relieved that no drool came out. So at least I'd evolved that much since third grade.

"So this is where they stick all the troublemakers," I said.

She looked up and smiled but seemed distracted. I was blocking the exit, and the crowd of people wanting to leave was growing restive behind me. I made one last stab. "I hope you're having a wonderful night," I said, which earned me a "Meh" and a giggle. I had no choice but to give up and move along, unless I wanted to bear responsibility for turning a gala into a Pamplona-style stampede.

Understand that I was never the type to fawn over anybody or dwell on what I could have done better. But I couldn't get the mystery blonde out of my head. I'm not sure if it was the fact that she was the most beautiful woman I'd ever met, her stunning black dress, or her nonchalant yet pleasant reaction to my inane dad joke. Something made me determined to talk to her again.

With my inner computer nerd playing wingman, I flew into action as Captain Cybersleuth. Time for non-creepy, perfectly innocent social media stalking. I looked at the charity Facebook page and website and couldn't find her in any of the photos. I pulled up guests and media I knew had been there, but again, she was nowhere to be found. After

No, pretty sure it was the full creepy kind . . .

exhausting every avenue I could think of within 48 hours, I called off the search and concluded that it just wasn't meant to be. (Thanks for nothing, fate, Cupid and Mark Zuckerberg.) I kicked myself that I didn't at least ask for her name which, in hindsight, would have helped greatly.

Almost a month passed. I kept busy at work and found myself just taking it easy one evening, catching up on emails and chilling out. Fighting a mild bout of FOMO, I flipped open my Instagram account. The first picture that popped up was a friend of mine . . . and in the background was the mystery girl. I nearly fell out of my chair. Of course she wasn't tagged, so I still didn't know her name, but at least now there was a possible link. I didn't want to just text my friend directly and ask him who she was, because who knew, it could be somebody he was dating. Or an ex. I needed to work out this riddle on my own. It only took another fifteen minutes of sleuthing before I struck gold and discovered who she was: Jacinta Kuznetsov. And she wasn't my friend's girlfriend or ex or anything else awkward. She was his producer. I found her Instagram profile and Twitter page.

Now I just needed to figure out how to make contact without looking like a creep. I also needed a better opening line than "so this is where they stick the troublemakers."

I sifted through her listed preferences and found she was a DJ. What a coincidence! I like music! Nope. Too much of a stretch. Just as well, since I found out later that she had filled her profile with fake info, anyway, and had no experience whatsoever in scratching records.

Hmm, maybe I just reach out and say hi. What's the worst that could happen? Check. I already knew that. But drool doesn't travel through computer keyboards, so I tapped out my first love letter to her:

Still hanging solo in the troublemaker section of charitable events? Or have you moved up to wedding crashing? Enter.

I then sat and waited anxiously for a reply, which didn't come for three days. What finally landed was just a light-hearted, witty retort that induced a mild chuckle and embarked us on a five-month battle of the brains until we discovered we would both be in the same city for the same event at the same time. We HAD to finally meet in person to see if the chemistry was as strong without the safety net of a keyboard.

We kept it casual and light. Jacinta met me and a few friends at a nightclub at the Bellagio Hotel. After quickly discovering there was no way to actually converse over the bass-thumping dance music, we decided to break away to a quiet bar to enjoy a drink and get to really know each other.

I felt this overwhelming urge to learn everything about her, but I didn't want to delve too deep on a first date and come across as pushy. So I asked about her career and fished for any similarities. The conversation was pretty routine for first-round pleasantries—when all of a sudden, Jacinta dropped a bomb.

"Ugh!" she groaned. "You ask the WORST questions. Ask something interesting." I was taken aback. Not exactly sure what to say, slightly offended and paralyzed with shock, I finally mustered a response.

"Sorry?"

To which she replied: "Seriously. These questions are so boring."

Well, excuuuuuuse me, Oprah Winfrey. I let her insult sink in for a moment and suggested perhaps she could contribute to the conversation, then. At which point, it all went downhill. I remember thinking, *This is not a nice person. Who would say that? Why am I still here?*

So finally I just said, "Why don't we call it a night? If you're not interested in being here, then there's no point." I walked her to the elevator and said good-night without eye contact or so much as a fist bump, I was so deflated. A little heartbroken, surprisingly. The person I'd built this rapport with over the past five months was completely different from the one I just met. Maybe I wasn't ready to open up that much to somebody yet.

As I walked away, I heard her call after me: "Jonathan!"

I just threw my hands up in the air and kept walking.

I sat in my car for a good twenty minutes, replaying where I had gone wrong, how something so full of promise had ended up derailing so badly. Was I being too sensitive out of pride? Was she legitimately not a good person? What was my friend who she worked for going to say? Ugh. Let the social awkwardness begin. I had always been great at keeping my private life very private. And now, one of my friends was no doubt going to hear about the Diva of all Diva moments that I just had. Perhaps a little damage control was in order.

I texted Jacinta, apologized for my behavior, and explained that wasn't who I am, that I honestly was not sure what had happened back there. After a few moments, she responded, saying she, too, was confused and it was not her intention to offend me. She was trying to be funny.

At that point, I discovered I had it all wrong: She was not some stone-hearted jerk who couldn't care less about the feelings of others. In truth, Jacinta was the most sarcastic person I'd ever met and, much like me, thrived on taking advantage of even the most intimate of moments to get a laugh. We could literally be the same person. . . .

You already have a twin! Ha ha

We decided that it was worth starting fresh and attempted a new first date the following night. I promised to drop the drama and she pledged to set aside the sass. It turned out to be the beginning of something truly special.

Jacinta's life was in Toronto, and mine was wherever Drew and I happened to be filming any given month. Jacinta and I knew it would take some flexibility and complex travel maneuvering to ensure we could spend as much time as possible with each other, but we promised never to let the time apart be considered a negative thing. It actually worked out well, because we pack a lot into our time together, and absence really did make our hearts grow fonder.

I remember when Jacinta planned to come see me in New York. It was her first big trip to come visit me on location. She was a little nervous, so I created a website called convincingjacinta.com, where I cryptically laid out a series of clues about the adventures that awaited. She loved the mystery and didn't come close to guessing what the activities were. (A medley of visits to the Central Park zoo, an escape room, an archery range, and one of the oldest pizza joints in the city.) One thing I quickly came to know about Jacinta was that if she had to choose between her love for me and her love for pizza, she'd have to think about it.

Every minute we spent together left us wanting to spend even more. We'd alternate who got to plan each reunion. We relished the challenge of keeping it a secret and surprising the other with the most random, unique experience we could think up. We'd also leave hidden notes in each other's suitcases, which sometimes wouldn't be discovered for weeks. We both love the little signs of affection and, even more than the grand gestures, I think they're the key to making a long-distance love work. A carefully conceived gift out of the blue shows how closely you listen to your partner's story, picking up the subtlest clues to recreate a favorite memory or fulfill some long-ago wish. Finding a sweet note in a coat pocket is a reminder that you're thought about, missed, considered when you're not around.

It was only six months into dating when it was my turn to plan a trip to Vancouver with Jacinta. Highlights included taste-testing the world's best bagel in Granville Island and a run through Stanley Park, which was as selfless a romantic concession as it could be, since she loves running and I hate it. I hate it more than blind dates. The *pièce de résistance* had us picking up a small boat and sailing to various nearby islands in search of the home my parents lived in before I was born. It was something I'd always wanted to do, and Jacinta shared the same excitement. It was important to her, because it was important to me. That was when I knew.

I was in love with this woman.

I'm not the type of person to hold in my feelings, but with a lifetime's worth of relationship perspective behind me, I knew exactly what my feelings meant. That night at dinner, I spoke those three little words again. Only now I understood their true meaning. And of course, as if to only mess with me just a little bit more, it took Jacinta three days to respond. But you know what, I'm fine with it, because she's got my attention for the rest of my life.

I even agreed to run a marathon with her.

Jacinta

Before I met Jonathan, I was in a comfortable stride in my life. I was enjoying my career and my friends, family bonds were strong, and I had time to volunteer, dance, make pottery, travel, go hiking, and otherwise pursue my passions. I was actively disengaged from dating. I had my own momentum and didn't want a relationship keeping me from what I wanted to do.

My parents always taught me to live boldly, with integrity and self-respect, and that you will get what you give. My attitude toward life and love was lovingly described by family as being "very independent" (and not-so-lovingly referred to by friends as "deliberately self-sufficient with the determined freedom of a wrestler stuck in a headlock." Or something like that).

That's where Jonathan came in.

It proved impossible to convince myself otherwise of what was so obvious when we first began seeing each other. Things didn't feel forced or unnerving; they felt joyful and easy. He was smart and quick-witted, qualities I needed in someone so I wouldn't fall asleep at the table and dream of pizza, sweatpants, and Netflix. I adored the moments I didn't have to explain myself because he already understood and the little jokes between us that would have us giggling to ourselves. His character and integrity showed in everything he did. He felt like home. I no longer felt scared to make a leap with someone. Although I *was* scared to say "I love you" first. (A glass of wine or three might have made me dreamily say it to him, but a fake sneeze covered that right up.)

Moving over to work with his company, in the same field I was before, is a benefit we are fortunate to have. Career and passions are very important to me, and I am thankful I have a man who respects and values that. I love being able to talk about the weird world we work in, like why all PAs have to be awkward, or they aren't a real PA. We smile and talk about how easy it was to bridge our lives together when there are so many moving parts. Jonathan's nonstop work schedule is crazy, but somehow fun always manages to find us.

I now know a relationship is about sharing passions and pursuits, not compromising them. I am sincerely grateful for the man he is, and that I get to have him in my life. I never expected to meet someone who had the same outlook on life with the same determination to make the most of it. Which feels really good. And nothing like a headlock.

LOVE WASN'T ON
MY RADAR. IT
WASN'T EVEN ON MY
MIND. I DON'T KNOW
WHAT I WAS LOOKING
FOR . . . BUT I'M
GLAD IT FOUND ME.
—Drew

Linda

Drew

Comments by Jonathan

ROMANCE, PART II

You would've broken it.

I f the researchers who famously calculated how many words the average person speaks in a day (15,000!) had hooked me up to their electronic trackers, I definitely would have landed on the upper end of their grading curve.

Whether it's small talk, a deep discussion, or some quick-fire banter, I like to keep the convo going. And let's not forget that it takes some silver-tongued talent to negotiate million-dollar deals, entertain audiences, and keep Jonathan in line. To be honest, thinking way back, the only time words failed me was when I wanted to make an impression on a member of the opposite sex. If my radar locked on an attractive girl with that "je ne sais quoi," I would hang back so long—trying to craft the perfect ice-breaker—that she would be gone by the time I was ready to say hello. Or, I would just walk right up and blurt out whichever words made it from my brain to my mouth first. But on October 23, 2010, after years of refining my approach, I concocted the perfect six-word combination to make contact.

"Hey, where'd you get that water?"

I was backstage at a Fashion Week event in Toronto during our first year of filming *Property Brothers*, and the random stranger holding the bottle of H_2O I wanted was, it just so happened, gorgeous. The moment I walked in, I heard her infectious laugh and could tell by her personality that this was somebody I wanted to know. She flashed a dazzling smile and told me where to go. For the water, I mean. Then she sealed both our fates with a meaningful question of her own:

"Where'd you get that pizza?"

I try not to be obvious when it comes to flirting. Jonathan, Pedro, and JD dubbed me "The Robot" when I was in ninth grade because I never showed much emotion. It used to take weeks, if not months, of angst and mental rehearsal for me to work up the nerve to even approach a girl I found attractive. At 32, I was long past that painfully awkward stage, but I still wasn't the type of guy to go in with guns blazing. I was more strategic. My m.o. was to start a conversation with some generic question or comment, keep it light, and see where it led. But, standing in front of this woman now waiting for me to tell her where I'd found the pizza, I was frankly awestruck. I'd never felt this kind of instant connection before. *Don't let her go,* urged the voice in the back of my head.

We introduced ourselves, but we both had official duties to attend to. I was in the show, and Linda was on patrol as the "fashion police," wearing a big badge and carrying a pad of tickets so she could cite fashion offenders. I escaped that fate, naturally.

I kept my eye out for Linda all night, making a point to say a word or two to her each time our paths crossed. When the event ended and everyone shifted to the after-party, though, I lost her.

Hopefully scanning the crowd at the second gathering, I kicked myself for not sparking up a great convo with Linda earlier. Now I couldn't get her out of my mind, while she probably already had me archived in a file labeled, "~~Tall Guy~~, Dry Mouth." *Robot*

I was on the verge of turning the after-party into my own private pity party when she appeared out of nowhere, like a magician without the smoke. She had this playful, vibrant energy that I could feel from halfway across the room, where she was . . . talking to some other guy. Damn. The one night I forgot to accessorize with a claymore from my sword collection. Good thing I'd studied improv. I would vanquish the interloper with my sharp wit instead.

I walked over and planted myself between Linda and my presumed rival, making an exaggerated show of rudely giving Linda my back as I pretended to be chatting up the guy. I played it off as a joke, which was my in. And, by the way, did I happen to mention that I was Tom Welling's body double on *Smallville*? Truth. So it couldn't be that bad of a view.

Linda wasn't offended, confirming my hunch that she shared my twisted sense of humor, and the guy she was talking to turned out to be just a good friend. Linda and I chatted here and there throughout the night about everything from volleyball to movies to the fact that she lived in Toronto and did drafting for an architectural firm. The most

I'm assuming she needed something for her nausea?

167

*Whoa, whoa. We were being gentlemen.
Maybe we should've charged for gas.*

important discovery was that she was seeing someone. I recall feeling disappointed, but still happy to have made a new friend since I was just starting out in Toronto, and she seemed like she would be a great tour guide. Linda's date that evening was her older sister, Wanda.

We still both had official mingling to do, so we agreed to stay in touch and went back to working the crowd. When Jonathan and I were ready to call it a night, there stood Linda waiting outside for a cab with her sister Wanda. We could not in good conscience let our new-found friends venture home in such an insipid fashion, so we offered them a ride. Linda later confessed that the only reason she broke the cardinal rule about never getting into a car with a stranger was because "there were two of us and we were pretty confident we could kick your butts if you turned out to be creeps."

When Jonathan and I wrapped up filming in Toronto, I invited Linda and her sister to the party we were throwing before heading home for the holidays. They were busy, but Linda asked me to let her know when I was going to be back in town so we could get together then. I remember turning to Jonathan and saying, "You know that cute, funny fashion police girl from the runway show? She's single now." And I was right.

We finally managed to have our first date on January 21, 2011. It was actually three dates in one, because a) I wanted to make sure she didn't get bored, and b) I wanted to delay saying good-bye for as long as possible without raising any alarm about a possible hostage situation. First, we went out for sushi, a favorite food we were happy to discover we had in common. Then it was on to a hot chocolate café

Linda had mentioned when we first met. After that, she had plans to go to her best friend's birthday party at a karaoke bar after the cocoa date-within-a-date, and I invited myself along. Hey, it was karaoke! She didn't object, and I figured fate was rooting for me when the guest of honor couldn't find his own party, and I got another 45 minutes of Linda time to myself. We crushed Lonely Island's comedy rap "I'm on a Boat" and smoothly sailed right into *Grease*, a transition that should not be attempted without emergency karaoke personnel on standby. For the record, I sang Sandy's part and Linda brought out her best Danny.

We've been inseparable ever since. (I'd say "attached at the hip," however my hips are at her shoulders, LOL.)

Lame as my water pickup line may have been, Linda truly was my oasis in the desert.

In theory, I should have had some swagger in the romance department. Even in the notoriously self-conscious teen years, I was totally at ease performing in front of a crowd, whether it was onstage in a high school musical or on the gym floor at a national karate championship. And I've always thrived under pressure and enjoyed the thrill of competition. When we went out to some club, I could be my talkative self as long as we were socializing and joking around, but when it reached the critical moment of asking a girl for her phone number or a date, I was like a deer in the headlights. I'd completely freeze.

I think I was emotionally scarred by a star on the girls' volleyball team when I was a freshman in high school. Tall and lean with short

Watching Drew try to flirt was like seeing a Ben Stiller movie play out before your eyes.

blond hair, she was popular in the athletics crowd. I spent a few months devising and discarding clever ways to get her to go out with me. I was on the boys' volleyball team, so I could suggest we practice together after school. Or I could ask her if she needed any help with her algebra homework, what with me being a numbers nerd and all. Because who wouldn't jump at an invitation to go on a math date? In the end, I ambushed her one afternoon outside the gym and mumble-stuttered my carefully crafted question:

"Will you go out with me sometime?"

"No thanks," she said. It wasn't mean so much as lightly dismissive, which in a weird way probably shredded my confidence much worse. If she had recoiled in horror and said something like, "Why would anyone go out with you, you hideous blob of protoplasm?" then at least I would have felt . . . acknowledged. Instead, I had all the impact of a dust mote.

The last thing I ever wanted to do was come across as desperate and/or delusional. I would fall in "like" with a girl, and instead of cranking up the charm, I'd find myself formulating an exit strategy to escape embarrassment or rejection before even approaching her in the first place. In my skewed logic, merely walking up to a girl to test the waters seemed like an invasion of her privacy, even in a crowded singles bar. When I forced myself to at least try, the result was always stilted. That reaction might have made some sort of sense if I'd been drawn to aloof supermodels who only dated music moguls, but my type was sweet girl-next-door or athletic and adventurous. My celebrity crushes were Tiffani-Amber Thiessen from *Saved by the Bell* and Sporty Spice. (Jonathan leaned more toward Christina Applegate or

Domo arigato, Mr. Roboto.

*Umm, Tyra was behind my college closet door!
(And by the way, thank you very much
Sports Illustrated, winter '97 swimsuit edition.*

Tyra Banks, whose posters he kept hidden in his room on the back of his closet door. Still might, come to think of it . . .

As soon as we hit the legal age (in Vancouver) of 19, Pedro, Jonathan, and I started hitting up a popular downtown nightclub called The Rage. With multiple levels and an aircraft hangar–sized dance floor, the club was massive, capable of holding over a thousand people. That had to improve our odds. The three of us looked like extras who wandered off the set of *A Night at the Roxbury*. Pedro and I dressed in tight, shiny shirts, while Jonathan was more likely to channel the violet suit/black turtleneck/gold chain look. And no, we weren't trying to be ironic, in case you were wondering. Whereas Jonathan and Pedro really played their parts, I merely dressed it. Even with my how-could-you-not-want-this outfit, I still felt out of place. I spent a lot of time standing by the bar drinking water and nodding my head to the beat of the music. The only pickup game I excelled at was on the basketball court.

Even though there were hundreds of presumably eligible women at The Rage on a weekend night, Jonathan and I would inevitably end up interested in the same one. Then, in some sort of strange bar scene deposition, we'd instantly claim we each had seen her first. More often than not this debate would carry on until the girl had disappeared into the crowd, or found another dance partner.

Jonathan insisted my dating downfall was that I was "too nice" and just needed to chill out.

*You'd always instantly enter the friend zone.
That's a one-way journey.*

Ugh . . . enter "The Coach."

When I was 21, I decided my best course of action was to challenge myself once a day to talk to a girl I didn't know in a manner that wasn't awkward. Though initially there was some rejection, I discovered that most women were more than willing to participate in a little idle chatter. As soon as that felt natural, I would try talking to two female strangers a day, then three, then four, and so on. I wasn't hitting on them; I was just trying to get myself to a point where one-on-one conversation would be easier. The conversations kept growing longer and the responses continued to get better. I discovered I already had the humor, the wit, and the social skills women wanted . . . I had just been lacking the confidence. Gradual exposure: That was the key. I think that approach is usually used to help people overcome their phobias of things like spiders, cottage cheese, or down escalators, not help someone get a date—but who cares? It worked. My theory might as well have been published in some relationship journal because I had personally proved it over the course of a couple of years and had more date offers on the table than I knew what to do with. My insecurity was banished. Delusions of grandeur took its place.

Drunk on my own success, now I was convinced I was some kind of relationship guru. I appointed myself the resident relationship expert among our friends, and proceeded to offer advice.

The main thing I was trying to do was help these guys so they didn't have to suffer through the same awkwardness that I had. I could see myself in them. I couldn't bear watching idly from the sidelines as my buddies fumbled. *Even when no one was actually asking for it.*

"Hey, don't you think you should ask her out?" I remember prodding our friend Jodi when I thought he ought to be making a move. My newfound soulmate Spidey-sense had sounded an alert that a potential love connection was within our strike zone . . . no one was going to become the 40-year-old virgin on my watch! I could see the girl in question was showing interest in Jodi when we struck up a conversation, but then he just shut down while I continued to talk.

"She said she was interested in rock climbing. You like rock climbing. Talk about that!" I suggested. "Really listen to what a woman says and take your cue from that," I added. I thought I had unlocked the Da Vinci Code here. The brain cells I reserve for minding other people's business were already registering Jodi and the outdoorsy stranger for wedding gifts. Could carabiners be engraved? Needless to say, Jodi got the date, and I was still the reigning champ of love/lust connections.

My cocky confidence even threw Jonathan off his game. No more playing the passive wingman for me. One night is still the stuff of legend in our guy-crew. We had all gone to a club to hang out and grab some drinks. I was standing with one of our friends when we noticed a striking brunette holding court nearby.

"How has Jonathan not noticed her?" I asked a buddy. The brunette seemed exactly his type: Tall and cute, with what sounded like a friendly, outgoing personality.

"Yeah," our friend replied, "wouldn't it be hilarious if he turned around and you were kissing her?"

"I could," I immediately responded. I was The Man, this sounded like a dare, and it would make Jonathan totally jealous. Of course I would do it.

"No, you couldn't," goaded our friend.

I was warming up the conversation with her friends but had my eye on her from the moment I got there. Months had passed and you still hadn't made a move . . . so I did!

"I guarantee I can get a kiss from her in five minutes or less," I announced as I made my way over to the unsuspecting brunette.

Within moments we were talking and laughing like BFFs. Jonathan turned around just in time to see the kiss. His jaw dropped.

Jonathan was understandably worried once I got the hang of flirting. My gain was potentially his loss. Women were starting to pick up on my confidence and signal their interest.

Save for one relationship that lasted around six months, though, I spent my 20s dating sporadically. I didn't want to waste time going through the motions with someone I knew wasn't "the one." I was VERY focused on work, and didn't have a lot of free time to begin with; I'd much rather spend it with the people closest to me or doing some activity I loved than on a dead-end date. Why shuffle my life around to fit in someone who wasn't going to be in it long-term? I wasn't unhappy or dissatisfied with my life at all, but I wondered if I was supposed to be. Had I grown accustomed to being single and so content with playing the field that I was at risk of locking myself into a lifetime of solitude? I found myself wanting a therapist's feedback for the first time in my life. My acting coach, Matthew Harrison, was the one to plant that seed. His philosophy was that all good actors

. . . and this is when you developed the idea that all women were giving you "Dreamy Eyes."

But I knew that you were still looking for that special somebody, you just had the bar set really high.

should regularly see a therapist because it can help you get in touch with your emotions, which in turn can help you with your craft, as well as in everyday life. The therapist I consulted offered reassurance when I wondered if I should be doing something different. Was my complacency normal?

If the status quo worked for me, she replied, then it was normal for me.

My first date with Linda erased every question, doubt, or disappointment I'd ever had about finding love. The fact that my family fell instantly in love with her, too, was no surprise, but still icing on the cake. She could finish our sentences and even beat us to the punch lines of inside jokes from our childhood. "Who *is* this girl and how does she know every funny anecdote I'm about to tell?" Jonathan asked me. Linda's sense of humor came with a zest for adventure and boundless energy that fed my own. The filming schedule of *Property Brothers* turned Jonathan and me into HGTV gypsies, moving from location to location every three to six months. What most people would likely see as a major obstacle to nurturing a relationship actually made Linda's and mine more romantic. Linda was able to work on the road and came along as we hopscotched from Austin to Toronto to New York, Vancouver, and Vegas.

Linda happily rolled with the communal living arrangement we usually had with Jonathan, his two dogs, assorted friends and family who might be visiting, plus our production team, crew members, and glam squad, who were constantly streaming through whatever house

Haters gonna hate!

we'd rented for the duration of our stay. You never knew whether our great room was going to be taken over for an all-day photo shoot, an impromptu hot-yoga session with friends, or a noisy midnight marathon of Cards Against Humanity. Linda is the kind of multitasker who can pay equal attention to a complicated graphic she's designing on her laptop and the video a crew member is insisting everyone stop to watch of a gajillion baby spiders scrambling off of a big spider being hit with a broom. (She was more alarmed by a glimpse of Jonathan in his gold lamé short-shorts: "I can't ever unsee that," she lamented.)

Wherever we are, Linda makes it her mission to find cool things to entertain us with and keep the adrenaline monkeys on our backs well-fed. Her spontaneity is contagious, and I've discovered that I can still work hard but actually have more fun doing so when I'm not as single-minded about it as I used to be. Like me, she's game for just about any physical challenge. Her competitive streak makes me half-wonder if we should get DNA testing to make sure we weren't closely related. We've taken trapeze lessons, played trampoline dodgeball, and completed firefighter and police fitness tests. (Always good to have a Plan B career-wise, LOL.) Sometimes I'll surprise her with something like a romantic date night doing an American Ninja Warrior challenge.

Even better, Linda also challenges me to take more risks emotionally, to check my tendencies to be analytical and regimented, and let go more often. She's the type of person who's always thinking of something special for people she cares about. I love finding funny little

I think she may actually be a ninja.

My philosophy is "If it tastes good, it must be good for you."

notes from her tucked in my suitcase, or watching her lost in concentration as she works on some amazing new artistic project. When we decided to have our big family Christmas in Maui last year, Linda made beautiful beach-themed stockings for everyone to hang.

She even coaxed out the hidden romantic in "the Robot." I found myself excited to find unique ways to surprise her—not easy when you're in love with a wildly creative one-woman think tank. Food has been a recurring theme. We're both gastronomes, though I'd have to say I'm definitely more the health nut.

Coming from a family that loves games and puzzles, creating scavenger hunts is one of my favorite things to do for Linda. Jonathan is always willing to lend his computer-geek skills to design a website that unlocks clues, or I'll just leave notes around the house for Linda to find while I'm away, leading her to a freezer full of every single flavor of Häagen-Dazs the store had in stock, or some other treat. I acknowledged her obsession with pizza by tracking down a pizza purse to give her.

For her birthday, I had jewelry custom-made to commemorate our relationship: The bracelet was engraved with the geographical coordinates of our first date, while the matching prism necklace depicted cities that were meaningful to us on each side.

You forgot to mention how you left the gift in an unmarked package in the overhead bin of an airplane and spent a week trying to get it back from Homeland Security. Sweet, sweet romance.
At least they didn't detonate it.

Having Linda by my side at the beginning of the television career I had wanted since I was a kid made it that much more exciting as all the hard work and struggles finally paid off. She became the cornerstone of my lifestyle, and I saw the potential to put her talents to work within the entertainment empire Jonathan and I were building. It didn't take long for us to bring her into the Scott Brothers fold as creative director.

Work for us never had been structured around a traditional eight-hour day, and never will be. It's just part of a lifestyle we've adapted to that intertwines work, play, and all the ordinary and extraordinary stuff in between in a way that makes the most sense on any given day.

Both of us have had to make compromises to be a couple. I've had to give up locking myself away to spend endless hours emailing and working on my computer, and Linda likewise sacrifices time indulging in extended benders of her favorite solo pastimes, like crafting, so that together we can enjoy a shared passion like Ping-Pong. She takes pleasure in a leisurely stroll, and I have to fight the urge to pick up the pace to get to the destination more efficiently. She's taught me to slow down once in a while and enjoy the little things in life. When Jonathan and I renovated the Scott family dream home we share in Las Vegas, he got the master bedroom in exchange for the private patio off the smaller bedroom Linda and I took. We turned the small outdoor space into our own little Parisian courtyard with potted plants, cobblestones, and a bistro table with chairs. No Jonathan (or his pups) allowed. I never would have thought I could be so peaceful just sitting and doing nothing until I had Linda sitting beside me.

As our sixth anniversary together approached, I called a restaurant several friends had raved about in Toronto and reserved a table for a special date night. Time alone is a luxury for us, and the sensual but whimsical vibe of Piano Piano spoke to us as much as the delicious Italian food. After we polished off our pasta and meatballs, Linda ordered carrot cake for dessert, knowing it's my favorite.

While we were waiting, the restaurant's soundtrack began playing one of our fave songs, "Marry Me," but Linda didn't notice that it was my voice coming through the speakers instead of Train. I'd spent weeks setting up the surprise, going to the studio to record it, and conspiring with the restaurant to play it as they wheeled out not Linda's dessert, but the custom one I had ordered: A beautiful, towering cake inspired by the cover of Linda's most-beloved Dr. Seuss book, bearing my promise for our future together—*Oh, The Places We'll Go*. The figurine atop the cake held a tiny balloon in one hand. A diamond solitaire engagement ring dangled from the other. Linda was still looking confused—"*What? I ordered carrot cake!*"—when I got down on one knee and, choking back tears of joy, asked her to be my wife.

If I had to choose one day of my life to live on endless repeat, it would be December 13, 2016, when the most incredible woman in the world said yes.

To me.

My grand plans to record the moment were undone by technical issues when the lighting proved inadequate for the hidden cameras I'd had installed in the restaurant, and the microphones picked up the stilted first-date conversation at a neighboring table instead of my proposal. Maybe the universe was sending me a message about oversharing.

THANK YOU! I don't think "I do" needs to be immortalized with a selfie. Ha ha.

The Robot, meanwhile, keeps yielding more and more to the romantic inside me. I'm the first to admit that the movie *Love Actually* makes me tear up. What gets me every time are the opening and closing scenes that create a collage of families and friends greeting each other at the airport. It reminds me of when I was a child and our whole family would get together to pick up relatives when they flew in. Holding welcome signs, flowers, and balloons. That pure, simple joy of coming together and belonging together.

Maybe it's because I've had way too much practice over the past twenty years, but we knew it would be quicker and easier for us to find and renovate our dream home than plan a wedding—though I'm not sure demo and drywalling fall under the duties bridesmaids are expected to perform. (Linda's up to fourteen already, and knowing how hard it is to get trades these days, maybe we have the bachelorette party involve sledgehammers and pry bars. Free demo labor!)

We quickly decided to buy our first house together in Los Angeles and began looking for a fixer-upper. There were about a thousand houses on the market that met our requirements and were in the neighborhoods where we were looking, but only ten were fixer-uppers that hadn't been touched. Everything else had had some kind of work done, which, in typical L.A. fashion, gave them an inflated price, which was all the more frustrating because we, in typical Scott fashion, were itching to do it all ourselves and ensure it was done right.

Linda and I toured all ten contenders in one day. When we stepped out of our car in front of a 1921 English Country–style house in Hancock Park, we both immediately had the same thought: This is the one. Aside from some 1960s shag carpet in the bedrooms, the house still maintained its original features and character, giving it a period feel

Ahem!! OK . . . maybe with a little help from Jonathan.

we were eager to preserve. Linda even wants to keep the original wall-paper in most of the bedrooms, plus the French poodle print adorning a powder room. My mom instantly recognized the pattern of dogs preening in front of vanity mirrors as the same wallpaper she had in her childhood home growing up in Toronto. No way were we keeping these self-absorbed poodles on the walls, but as I expected, the gears in Linda's head were already turning as she worked out some creative ways to repurpose them.

I'm excited because this is our first home together, and Linda and I are actually doing the design ourselves. Linda and I both love the idea of revitalizing the character and history of the home. We want every space to have conversation pieces, features that express our personalities. I've always fantasized about having a formal, Old World–style library, with floor-to-ceiling bookshelves filled with first editions of the classics I enjoyed as a child and other beautiful volumes. Linda's ultimate high would be an inspiring space to let her artistic side run wild.

It wasn't long after purchasing our new home and discovering how unique it was that we agreed it HAD to be filmed as a special. It was too amazing and too perfect a property to pass up capturing its transformation to share with our fans. But this place represents more than just a roof over our heads. This will be the house we live in when we get married; the first big stop in all the places we'll go. We want these walls to echo with the laughter and love of all the friends and family we hope will come visit.

And you can bet we'll be right there to meet them with signs at the airport.

SCENES FROM A 24/7 ROMANCE

Linda

After seven years of working and *staying* together, I'd say we've become pros at mixing business with pleasure. We take tremendous pride in our work and are grateful that together we can build something greater than ourselves. I'm incredibly lucky that we're on the same page . . . most of the time. Here are a few scenes from our day-to-day that show how the lines of our love life and work life are blurred—but that's okay because we don't color within the lines anyway. :)

Face Time

When we finally tuck into bed, the room temperature is set at a mutual 68 degrees (Drew loves the feel of cool, crisp sheets while I could sleep in a sauna). Drew is half on top of the sheets while I've rolled myself into a burrito. The sounds of Leon Bridges and Santo & Johnny softly play and we're both finishing up some work on our phones when . . . SMACK!

Drew dozes off and drops his phone. On his face!

After laughing at him (for a good minute), I plug his phone in, switch off the lights, and pass out myself.

Some nights we talk for hours in bed, while others we stay up late working. For us, being flexible works best when it comes to making sure we get quality face time. We tried the "no phones or laptops in bed" rule, and it lasted for all of three days—if even. Besides, how are we supposed to watch *The Walking Dead* or *Westworld*?!

Home Is Wherever I'm With You

We're on a beach somewhere. Lounging with our feet tangled together. The sun makes its way through tiny openings of a thatch umbrella. We hear the ocean waves, background chatter . . . and the *almost* therapeutic tapping on our keyboards. An hour passes without a word to each other when Drew decides it would be a gut-busting, brilliant idea to pour ice-cold water down my back. I let out a shriek that spills into laughter in the same breath.

Being on the road constantly has made us experts in turning wherever we are into our "homes" and "offices." In every new city, Drew and I take turns finding locations to set up shop. Whether it's a Ping-Pong bar or a restaurant with a bowling alley, a change of scenery reminds us that there's a world of beauty, humor, and inspiration around us, so LOOK UP! And yes, we actually enjoy working a little while on vacation. With toes in sand and blue skies as our backdrop, our heads are a little clearer to focus on passion projects and our big picture together.

Ain't No Mountain (Or Wall) High Enough

It's 6 o'clock, and we're in the car, heading to destination unknown! The only hints Drew gave me were to wear gym clothes and bring my A-game. We toggle between conversations about family, brainstorming new ideas on how to save the world, and belting out tunes. We're singing along to Marvin and Tammi when we pull up to a monolith of a building.

When we enter, my jaw drops—and IF I could do a celebratory backflip, I would! We spend the next four hours playing and training with an America Ninja Warrior! COOLEST DATE NIGHT EVER!

Drew is oftentimes more of an antic than a Romeo. So when it comes to "romantic" getaways or dates, ours are far from typical. But that's just the way we like it. Whether it's an escape room, an obstacle course gym, a pottery or cooking class, a flying trapeze, dancing, or an improv workshop, we take the time to do things the other person is crazy about because we're crazy about each other.

THE BEST OF FRIENDS CAN ALWAYS PICK UP
RIGHT WHERE THEY LEFT OFF . . . WHETHER
IT'S BEEN A DAY, A WEEK, OR EVEN A YEAR.
                            -Jonathan

Comments by Drew

BAND OF BROTHERS

The alarm goes off at 6:30 a.m. in a Los Angeles hotel room, coaxing me awake to quiet sounds of nature. Talk about false advertising! Thanks to the spreadsheet emailed by our full-time scheduler, I already know the week ahead is going be a far cry from any walk in the woods for Drew and me. A cry *in* the woods, maybe, since we won't be seeing a bed again until after 10 p.m.—tomorrow. I hit the snooze button, which prompts nature to nudge me a little less gently with the second alarm. The sweet warbling of songbirds could shift into the "dive o' death" scream of raptors—but there's still no way I am giving up that extra five minutes.

I know I wasn't the one experimenting with hair products.

So what exactly transpired between waking up in L.A. that particular Monday morning and finally going to bed again some 40 hours later in Galveston, Texas?

Take a peek:

MONDAY

7:00 a.m.   Travel to *Extra* (TV show)—hair/makeup ready

8:00 a.m.   Start shooting segment for *Extra*

9:00 a.m.   Wrap from *Extra*

9:00 a.m.   Travel to *E! Daily Pop*

9:30 a.m.   Arrive at *E! Daily Pop*

9:30 a.m.   Makeup and hair touch-ups

9:45 a.m.   Start shooting segment for *E! Daily Pop*

10:30 a.m.   Wrapped from *E! Daily Pop*

12:00 p.m.   Lunch meeting with Sony—pitch new show idea

1:30 p.m.   Meeting with Fox—pitch new show idea

3:00 p.m.   Meeting with agents

4:30 p.m.   Travel to hotel to change and freshen up

5:30 p.m.   Travel to *Guardians of the Galaxy 2* movie premiere

6:30 p.m.   Red carpet for *Guardians of the Galaxy 2* movie premiere

7:00 p.m.   *Guardians of the Galaxy 2* movie premiere

10:00 p.m.   Travel to LAX airport

12:30 a.m.   Flight to Nashville, TN (red eye)

TUESDAY

6:43 a.m.   Arrive in Nashville, travel straight to set

7:30 a.m.   Call in makeup and hair

8:30 a.m.   Start shooting segments for *Property Brothers* in Nashville

12:00 p.m.   Travel to *Buying and Selling* set in Nashville for afternoon shoot

12:15 p.m.   Phone interview with *People* magazine

12:30 p.m.   Phone interview with FoxNews.com

12:45 p.m.   Phone interview with *US Weekly*

1:00 p.m.   Phone interview with *E! Online*

1:15 p.m.   Makeup and hair touch-ups

1:45 p.m.   Starting shooting segments for *Buying and Selling* in Nashville

5:00 p.m.   Wrapped from shooting *Buying and Selling*

5:15 p.m.   Travel to Nashville airport

6:30 p.m.   Flight to Houston, TX

8:35 p.m.   Travel to Galveston, TX

9:45 p.m.   Arrive in Galveston, TX

Not me, mine's still good.

The rest of the week was fairly routine, with 12-hour days through Sunday, and a 20-hour work-a-thon on Thursday. All told, we totaled four flights, six interviews, ten business meetings, four public appearances, and a partridge in a pear tree. Somehow Drew managed to squeeze in a voice lesson and a guitar lesson, both via Skype, and we were each allotted a date night with our lovely ladies. But that's just what was pre-scheduled—stuff like unexpected delays on-site, answering a never-ending torrent of texts and emails, working on social media, playing with the pups, scarfing down the occasional handful of Skittles, shopping for design/reno goodies, and writing this book aren't included. Mind you, we're not complaining. We have a blast doing what we do.

It's what we *can't* do that gets frustrating.

And the biggest thing we can't do anymore is spend enough time with our friends. That's one void midnight Skittle raids can never fill.

Once we started appearing on TV, we began disappearing from the radar of acquaintances who struggled to deal with the new reality of our social lives. We went from being the up-for-anything fun guys you could always count on, to the would-love-to-do-anything fun guys who always had to wait until the last minute to see if they could do something. We were like that friend who marries a Velcro spouse who won't let you go out anymore. It wasn't that I didn't want to come over for dinner next Thursday (it makes my mouth water just thinking about a home-cooked meal) or that Drew wasn't in the mood to go rock-climbing in the desert next Sunday: We simply never know for

You've definitely tried though . . . sugar addict!

sure when our work day is going to end. Sometimes we wrap early and have the windfall of a free Saturday afternoon, and sometimes we miss an extreme full-contact game night because a basement flooded on one of our projects and I'm pulling a late one.

When down time becomes a scarce commodity, you treasure it a lot more, and high-maintenance relationships are the first to die of natural causes. Guilt-trippers and anyone allergic to spontaneity don't last long, either. And more than a few casual friends from the old days just stopped calling after hearing "No, sorry," too often. Others got angry or felt insulted.

But one core group flat-out refused to take it personally or get discouraged; they were the ones who would let a thousand apologetic no's roll off their backs and still come back and ask for the 1,001st time if we wanted to hang out.

Drew and I have been tight with same crew of guys since we were young teenagers. Over the years, we've seen each other through some of life's greatest joys and deepest sorrows, all of our histories and hopes welding together to form this unbreakable bond. Counting JD, our band of brothers—aka the Usual Suspects—numbers seven.

JD was always cool and mysterious. He had his own room down in the basement when we were growing up, and we were dying to know what was happening down there . . . but were deemed too annoying to gain entry. He must've been living the high life, because all the rules that applied to Drew and me up in our bedrooms were abandoned when it came to JD. How did he get to sleep in on weekends and avoid daily bedroom cleanliness checks? I smell a double standard!

As we got less annoying—or maybe he just got more resigned to it—JD shifted more into the wise big brother role, offering us guid-

Or at least an idiot. Ha ha.

ance and advice about the ways of life. Girls, music, hobbies, girls. We flunked the girl tutorial repeatedly, but JD never gave up trying.

I remember he had a comedy troupe called YFG (they would never tell anybody what it stood for) that performed locally to sell-out crowds. I would watch JD on stage and see the audience laughing uncontrollably and think, *WOW, he is good!* My assumption that he was a genius was further confirmed when we were riding in the car and he would be singing along to the music. How on earth did he know the words to all of the songs? He MUST be some kind of genius . . . or perhaps an idiot savant. He went full goth as a teenager, and people kept telling him he looked like Bon Jovi with eyeliner. Many years later he met a girl who was a professional Liza Minelli look-alike, and before long, JD's Bon Jovi look was adapted just enough for him to pull off performing as an Adam Lambert impersonator. Then he added David Bowie. We had no idea JD was such a great singer. Yet another one of his hidden mysteries that left us wondering where he learned such skills. Perhaps it was on a "walkabout" during one of the two times he moved to Australia. We'll never know, but when he was gone, we missed the heck out of him and would make him goofy videos for the holidays, even interviewing his friends for little snippets.

Regardless of how mysterious and unknowable he sometimes seemed, JD always showed up to offer his support when we needed it most. He moved with me to Las Vegas, and likewise to the lonely out-post of Grande Prairie with Drew to lend support in any way he could. JD set the loyalty bar high for the band of brothers who followed him.

The founding member of our gang was Pedro, our brother from an Iranian mother and chief co-conspirator in a 25-year string of pranks

We were laughing so hard on the bike ride to school at the thought of the first teacher who would use the freshly sealed toilets.

gone wild, stunts gone sideways, and common sense gone AWOL. Pedro could always run fast and stay cool in a crisis, talents that served him well in our youth. He bore witness to my earliest misadventures in plumbing and landscaping, which occurred at separate times but in the same unlucky place—our high school in Maple Ridge.

The first happened one spring day when we snuck into the empty school building to put plastic wrap over the toilet bowls. Teachers were on strike, so classes were canceled, and the facility was sitting there vacant, just begging to be pranked. As I went to lift the seat and wrap the first bowl, I noticed a pipe sticking up from the back of the toilet. It had a cap with a screw just staring right at me. Curious, I of course proceeded to unscrew it. Almost instantly there was a liquid explosion, then a geyser of water shot up and began spraying everywhere. Pedro, Drew, and I started yelling at each other as I tried to make it stop. I was pressing on the pipe as hard as I could, but the pressure was too strong. Everything seemed to happen in slow motion. I then noticed that the screw cap had landed in the toilet . . . and was rolling down the hole to the bottom of the bowl. With no time to think about how disgusting being this intimate with a public toilet was, I reached deep into the bowl and grabbed the screw. I managed to get the cap back on and re-threaded the screw. As I glanced around thinking, *Will anybody notice?*, I heard footsteps approaching and the principal's voice shouting "What the hell is going on in here?" There was no hiding the 90 gallons of water that had sprayed all over the room. I simply replied, "This toilet could have killed me! You need to get these checked out by a plumber," and we took off.

The next morning, the principal called the house while we were still in bed. Dad answered.

"Mr. Scott, are Jonathan and Andrew up yet?" the principal demanded.

"No, they're sleeping," Dad replied.

"Well, wake them up, because they vandalized the school yesterday!"

"That can't be right," Dad replied. "What was damaged?"

The principal hesitated. "Well, there was quite a bit of water that had to be mopped up and there was plastic film on some of the toilets."

Dad put him on hold and came to rouse us.

"Boys, did you vandalize the school yesterday?"

"No! It was an accident."

"Okay, go back to sleep."

Dad got back on the phone and gave the principal a piece of his mind for falsely accusing his sons, then hung up. The principal then tried calling Mom at work, and she ripped an even bigger strip off him for going behind Dad's back when he had already dealt with it. He also got an earful of indignant Farsi when he dialed Pedro's house. Not surprisingly, the school didn't call home anymore. We were good kids. But even good kids get up to a little harmless mischief from time to time.

I learned a valuable life lesson: Never mess with plumbing unless you know what you're doing.

Lesson #2 came when Pedro, Drew, and I got on the school librarian's last nerve—she hated noise and obnoxious teenagers, which crossed us right off her Christmas list. The principal ordered us to

Which hand did you reach down the toilet with? Remind me never to shake it again.

spend the weekend weeding the massive garden out front of the school. If done properly, it would have been about a 14-hour job—most of the plants were weeds. Then I had a brilliant idea: There were bags upon bags of wood chips stored around the back of the school, and we could just pour those all over the garden and cover the weeds in about an hour. Mulch hides anything if you've got enough of it. I bet even Rome could have looked finished in a day if they had enough mulch to dump on the city. The next morning, the principal walked around with us, astonished at how great the gardens looked. He declared that our punishment was over and we had paid our dues. By lunch that day, all the weeds had popped back up. Fortunately we had already received a full pardon. But at least the wood chips provided a nice contrast.

Further proof that Pedro was the soldier you wanted with you in the foxhole came in Banff, where the three of us got summer jobs at the Banff Springs Hotel right after graduation. There were tons of activities to enjoy outdoors, including rollerblading, hiking, and the occasional game of basketball. It was during one of those games that I fell victim to a flurry of Drew's elbows, which left me with a deep gash over my eyebrow that was bleeding like crazy.

Because we were self-reliant idiots, we didn't call an ambulance, nor did we want the expense of a cab, so we hustled on foot to the ER with rags pressed against my wound. By the time we got there, my shirt looked like I'd bought it at the Chainsaw Massacre Consignment Store. I finally stopped bleeding, but the cut was going to need stitches. We signed in and took our plastic seats in the bustling waiting room.

Well, you shoulda jumped higher for the rebound. I was on your team!

WE COULD BE BEACHSIDE IN MYKONOS
OR KNEE-DEEP IN MANURE ON THE RANCH—BOTH
WOULD BE EQUALLY HILARIOUS AND MEMORABLE
WITH FRIENDS LIKE THESE.
-Jonathan

You mean sixty?

And wait we did. New arrivals kept coming in and getting called ahead of me. Nobody looked as dramatically injured as I did, but maybe they had impressive internal injuries. We waited some more.

Emergency rooms are always exciting when Hollywood handles the plot line and set decoration, but most of the real ones I've been in (maybe six?) are as dull as a vintage issue of the crochet magazines that were lying around. I wasn't being upstaged by any gurneys racing past with sympathetic victims of freak spear-fishing accidents, but I wasn't making the triage nurse's Top 20 list, either. When I asked how long it would still be, she said I wasn't an emergency, so please sit down. Pedro shot me a glance that said, *Trust me*. Then, without a word, he grabbed my brow between his thumb and forefinger and reopened my wound, producing an impressive blood geyser. I was immediately hustled into a treatment room and sewn right up. There are SO many more tales of adventure I could share about our mishaps with the one and only Pedro, but that could fill another book.

The only other member of our main crew who dates back to the good old high school days would be Toni. He had muscles on muscles, a heavy English accent, and was the only friend of ours able to out- "pec pop" Drew. On his own, he apparently was a Don Juan and the women fell all over him, but around us he seemed so shy it was painful. Maybe he didn't want to give away his secrets. Many days were pleasantly wasted away on the court playing ball, and even more evenings at house parties working on our smooth talk. Toni was the worst wingman because once a girl met him . . . well, there was no sense in me even trying. We were so happy to attend his recent wedding, where he proved once and for all that he did meet a beautiful woman and must have said the right thing.

Then there's Brad. None of us liked Brad in the beginning. He was the annoying, smart-ass weirdo who lived at the end of the hall in our U Calgary dorm. He was the only student on our floor who had his own room . . . because no one would live with him. One night I was sitting in the common area watching some suspense movie when Brad came in and turned the channel to hockey.

"Oh, I was watching that," I said, in case he hadn't noticed me SIT-TING. RIGHT. THERE. Brad then spoiled the surprise ending of the movie, adding, "It's not worth it, anyway."

This guy is a monster, I thought. *Why would anyone do that?*

I ran into him not long after that, and Brad acted like nothing had happened and struck up a conversation. I don't hold a grudge, so I let go of the spoiler assault, and we ended up hitting it off. Need a clever insult? Brad was like a Pez dispenser of them. We eventually realized that he may lack a filter, but is as genuine and loyal as they come. He's a talented golfer and hockey player and never ended up using his archaeology degree before becoming an investment adviser. But hands down he's the smartest guy we know . . . at least when *Jeopardy* is on.

We are very open and honest about everything—except one event that we vowed never to speak of again: The Brooks High School magic show. When I was trying to turn magic into a full-time career, Brad's mom asked me if I would perform at her daughter's high school grad-uation celebration in their small town a few hours away. I was typically doing larger venues or more intimate evenings, but I didn't want to let Brad's family down. His mom said they had a budget of $450. I didn't want to be rude, but it cost more just to pay my dancers and haul my props there. I tried to wriggle out of it, but I could tell Brad's mom would be heartbroken. I decided to absorb the loss and put on the

DREW: "Band of Brothers"
seems quite appropriate
as everywhere we'd travel,
people would stop us,
thinking we were some
rock band.

JONATHAN: Yeah, they assumed I was the lead singer and Drew was just the key grip. Wait, no, that was Simpson. Ha ha.

show. She said they had a big auditorium that had been updated, and that it had the stage, lighting, and curtain I needed, and could handle all my tech needs, too.

I pulled up the day of the show to discover I would be performing on the floor of a concrete hockey arena with cut-open black garbage bags for curtains, a lone floodlight as a lighting system, no projector, and an audio system so ancient I had to cut and splice in my MiniDisc player. Just when I thought it couldn't get worse, the students started to arrive. A good third of them were absolutely wasted. The boys cat-called my dancers when they came on stage and booed and hollered when they left.

For my first illusion, I was supposed to make my grand entrance by suddenly appearing inside a large empty phone booth–like box rotating about 5 feet above the stage. At the climax of the routine, just before I was to make my grand appearance, the janitor was leaving for the evening and decided to turn off the power. The lights went dark and other than a few kids in the front row straining to make me out, nobody could see anything. Yet, oddly, the music kept playing. (What's that saying . . . if a magician appears in the middle of a pitch-black arena, does anybody notice? In this situation, the answer was a resounding NO.) Brad's mom managed to get the lights back on, but other than a few sympathy claps, nobody was impressed.

I jumped down off the prop and, thanks to the sheen of condensation on the arena floor from the humidity of all the people, I proceeded to slip and fall on my butt in a bad way. I hopped back up and played it off with a joke . . . but there was no saving this show.

This hardly even scratches the surface of why it became The Performance That We Will Never Speak of Again. My worst experience ever

Wait, I thought he was a geology major.

in front of a live—though only partially coherent—audience. If I had to do it all over again, of course I would. I did it for *Brad*.

Brad's biggest contribution to our crew was Jodi, a fellow archae-ology major (or so I thought, until I found out he was a geography major) who also didn't use his degree to become the next Indiana Jones. Jodi has worn many hats and even worked with Drew and me as a flight attendant for a while— those were some hilarious flights.

Jodi is the guru of all things music. Knows every song, every mel-ody, and every lyric from the Jazz Age forward. He can un-garble the Spanish words to La Bamba and the English ones to Blinded by the Light. He is fluent in Bob Dylan and can probably tell you the name of the guitar player for the Red Hot Chili Peppers' 1992 tour. His ridiculous ability to retain is not just limited to music though . . . he's an all-around storehouse of useless information that has proven time and time again to be not-so-useless.

Jodi is also a living, breathing copy of Lonely Planet. The dude researches everything about any place we go to. No need for Google or TripAdvisor—Jodi's reviews are ten times better. It's always the perfect mix of party life, culture, and the bizarre. Usually if we were planning a trip, he was the first one we'd call. And before we knew it, everybody wanted to come along for the ride. This was what started our unofficial ritual of taking a couple of guys' trips per year. It didn't matter if we were in Munich for Oktoberfest or at some hole in the wall in Edmonton, Jodi would work out an incredible itinerary with

Are you sure it wasn't geology he was taking?

ON MANY OF MY EUROPE TRIPS I WAS MISTAKEN
FOR A LOCAL, AS I HAD LONG HAIR AND A DARK TAN.
I GUESS I LOOKED LIKE AN ITALIAN GANGSTER . . .
WITH A CANADIAN ACCENT.

-Jonathan

We just won't rely on Jodi to book the hotels after the Barcelona incident of 2006.

Yeah, "roach motel in red-light district" is not my preferred home away from home.

ideal photographic backdrops and once-in-a-lifetime experiences. Over time as wives, babies, and demanding jobs came along, the trips dropped down to once a year, then every other year, then eventually to nothing more than a fond memory. Our last official one with the whole group was probably Europe around 2008, but I did travel to Munich with Jodi and a couple buddies in 2015 to soak up some beer, dance on some tables, and rock the lederhosen. As usual, Jodi figured out ways to keep us all entertained, and in return I covered as many bratwurst and sauerkraut dinners as he could consume. I've been fortunate enough to see more of Jodi in recent years than anyone else, mainly because of his flexible schedule, ability to still get cheap travel, and because I'm usually working in cities that he's always wanted to visit. It's really a perfect storm that has continued to keep us close after all these years.

Simpson is our resident key grip (entry-level production position). He always sits quietly in the background, formulating his plan to take over the world—or at least take the rest of us down with him if he doesn't. If anything embarrassing happens, though, Simpson is always the one who has somehow caught it on camera. For such a funny, caring guy, *man*, he has a dark sense of humor. If anybody could to take us down with dirt, it would be Simpson. His photographic evidence will put us all away.

You'd better hope none of those pics ever surface! Haha. Umm, there are WAY more compromising photos of you.

Mike also joined the gang through Brad and the U Calgary archaeology program, but unlike the other guys, his degree did pay off. (Though not in a career, but by introducing him to his archeologist wife, Andrea.) Mike's most recognizable trait is that he has the loudest laugh, and if it weren't for his successful career in IT recruitment, he could easily do voice-over work for Fran Drescher. Anyway, like everyone else in the crew, he has a passion for travel. He just takes his a little farther than the rest of us. Mike owns more sets of lederhosen than the Vienna Boys' Choir. Oh, and the tasseled knee socks to complete the look. Fortunately, he's lived for many, many years just outside Amsterdam, which is no more than a quick day trip to prime yodeling spots in Bavaria or Switzerland.

Mike was in his element when we decided to host one of our Usual Suspects reunions in Munich during Oktoberfest. Drew still has PTSD from that trip as he's not much of a drinker to begin with, but beer he especially can't stand—not the taste, not the smell, and not sitting in a beer tent packed stein-to-stein with loud, rowdy people whose sole purpose in being there is to consume as much beer as humanly possible. The more beer they drink, the more difficulty they have with their hand-eye-mouth-giant stein coordination, which means that beer inevitably gets sloshed, spilled, and sometimes intentionally poured on innocent bystanders—Drew being one of them. A bunch of our group were overzealously "cheersing" when one of the mugs broke, which dumped an entire beer in Drew's lap. Drew looked so miserable. Sadder even than my Yorkie, Stewie, getting a bath. Quickly conjuring up pure genius, Jodi and I instantly executed a plan to make sure Drew wasn't feeling left out: We each poured our own beers on our own crotches, and soon everybody else at the table

You mean I have been upholding it. I think I'm the only one who does this?!

followed suit. We may have stolen the idea from *Billy Madison*, but this was the kinda dedication we had to the group. In the end, we were successful in making ourselves reek of beer, but unfortunately we did not make Drew any happier. Meh, it was worth the try. All for one and one for all, or however that saying goes (Jodi would know). It was part of our Guy Code.

The main tenet of our unwritten but unanimously embraced Guy Code is to ~~humble~~ ourselves before our fellow man. Guy Code demands that you immediately report any embarrassing thing that happens to or because of you, sparing no detail. We've been (upholding) this for almost 20 years now. *humiliate*

Drew is the most entertaining player in this game, by far. But it's only fitting. He's the best at keeping in touch with everyone and bringing us all up to speed on who's doing what. It's not uncommon in those reports for Drew to include the embarrassing details of some brain fart moment that is still fresh in his mind. And being able to ridicule him is one of life's greatest pleasures, made even better when he supplies the ammunition himself. It's the next best thing to actually witnessing him trip over his suitcase getting off an airport shuttle and doing a face-plant into the bushes in front of LAX, for example.

The friendship we all share isn't just about fun vacations and reminiscing over good times. They're a second family—the people you trust can see you at your worst and still love you, the ones who show up

First of all, the wheel got caught, and secondly, the driver stopped like 2 feet from the curb!

when you're hurting without being sent for. We know they have our backs no matter what, and we have theirs.

When one of the guys went through a very sad divorce, he was in such rough shape afterward that he wasn't eating or sleeping, but would never ask for help. He fell into such a negative space for so long that everyone began getting compassion fatigue and distancing themselves rather than risk being dragged down with him. Not me. Not Drew.

As the first Valentine's Day since the divorce approached, Drew took him to the airport, stood in front of the departures board, and announced: "You pick anywhere on this board and we're going away for a week. My treat. We're going to relax, have some fun." The friend chose Maui. When they got there, though, the friend seemed to get worse. At the beach one afternoon, Drew noticed an odd tattoo on our friend's side.

"What's that?" he asked.

"It's the Hawai'ian islands," the friend answered. "It's where we got married."

Drew called him a jerk for not saying anything before, and they ended up laughing at the whole tragicomedy of the situation. Healing took time, but the friend did find his way back to happiness.

What makes these friendships endure is our ability to always pick up right where we left off, whether it's been days, or months, or even years. We give each other permission to just resume; we love letting the story continue to naturally unfold without demanding explanation.

What these friendships have taught us about loyalty has helped shape our businesses and inspired us to keep pushing our creative boundaries further. Taking a cue from Adam Sandler, who often hires

NOTHING WRONG WITH A GROUP OF GROWN MEN
GIGGLING DANGEROUSLY CLOSE TO THE POINT OF
PEEING. OKAY, MAYBE PAST THE POINT ONCE.

-Jonathan

friends or people he would like as friends at his Happy Madison production company, we make a conscious effort to surround ourselves with people who feed our souls in our professional lives just as we do in our personal ones.

It's a no-brainer to recruit our friends to work for our company, since they are guaranteed to have the qualities we value most, or we wouldn't have admired them in the first place. Linda and Jacinta both have talents that dovetailed with our creative needs, and we're optimistic that over time we'll be able to slowly pull in the expertise of all the Usual Suspects, too. Brad has already analyzed our investment portfolio, Jodi has shot a bunch of hilarious social pics for us, Mike has recruited technical positions for our businesses, Pedro has worked as general contractor on several of our real estate projects, and of course JD has worn many, many hats throughout the years. Team Scott is made up of people who are as passionate and unconventional as we are. Wherever we happen to be living at any given time, our house turns into Grand Central Station, and everyone makes themselves at home. Jacinta and I have jars of Swedish fish, Skittles, and other favorite candies always lining our snack counter, and over at Drew and Linda's, if they start making crepes for breakfast, they know better than to assume that it'll just be the two of them digging in. (Crepes are a favorite among everybody in our circle.) Colleagues are constantly picking up or dropping off something, and newfound friends from local trades we hire on the shows as well as peers in the industry quickly become part of the fold. Being open and flexible keeps the vibe fun. There are people in the industry notorious for issuing instructions that no one approach "the talent" without permission, but that's not the kind of bubble we'd ever want to live in.

One of the best parts of being a nomad is meeting so many people and making new friends wherever we set down for a few months. Doing *Property Brothers* and *Buying and Selling* this year in Nashville was especially fun since we're huge country music fans and have managed to meet even more people on the country scene since recording a few songs of our own. Being on location in such a great city has its perks because more friends pay impromptu visits. Barb, one of my dearest friends from my old WestJet days, is a gifted photographer who'll pop into town every so often with her cameras just to play. Spending a few hours with her is always unexpected, absolutely hilarious, and so fulfilling. We'll snap just as many beautiful, professional nature pictures as we do ridiculous, embarrassing, immature ones of each other. It's really the best way to recharge when my battery is down to a single bar in the middle of a month-long stretch without a day off. And when that month becomes two, I feel like I just won the lottery if a text appears from Brad or Jodi or any one of the Usual Suspects, who all know better than to ask what our schedule looks like.

Instead, they tell us they're on their way, and will be waiting wherever we are and whenever we're ready.

A BROTHER'S VIEW OF HIS BROTHERS

JD

Anyone who has been an older sibling knows there are many different levels to that position. Sometimes you are a teacher, sometimes you are a friend, and other times your job is simply to **GIVE THEM A HARD TIME.** When we were young, I felt that need to protect my little brothers from whatever came at us, although there were times where the opposite was true, and that fearless duo came to my defense. Their growth over a lifetime has been something wondrous to behold. From awkward (and occasionally irritating) teens to **BRILLIANT TITANS OF INDUSTRY,** they have proven that hard work and dedication to a dream can pave the way to success. It has been said that you can't be yourself on television, which has been proven wrong in the case of our family. My brothers have created an empire based around their talent, **GENUINE PERSONALITIES,** and commitment to fans. And here is a little gem of information not everyone knows: I was actually their first renovation/design client. In filming a sizzle video for a new show called *Rock Your Garage*, my brothers needed to make over a room in 24 hours to highlight their skills. They chose my living room for that project, which ultimately led to the shows you see today. Everything happened for a reason and when it was supposed to.

Comments
by Jonathan

TV WORLD

I was in the kitchen of the Galveston home I was flipping for *Brother vs. Brother* when a loud crash upstairs
interrupted a scene we were shooting about my alarming
discovery that the tile I planned to use along an entire wall
couldn't be cut to fit without crumbling. "CUT!" the director ordered—meaning the scene, unfortunately, not my tile.
No one bothered to go investigate the crash, because after
years spent working on construction sites, you can generally
tell the cause of random mishaps just by the noise. This was
likely just a ladder getting knocked over.

Once the commotion subsided, the cameras started rolling

again, and I had to relive my tile trauma showing the same surprise, disappointment, and light-bulb moment of how to fix it that I'd had when I first learned about it.

Was I acting? Yes, of course I was. Television is visual: at its best when it's showing instead of telling. The goal is to engage and entertain an audience, not put them to sleep while we stand around and literally watch paint dry.

Was the tile situation real? Yes, 100 percent. We don't create problems—we fix them, whether the cameras are rolling or not.

So where, then, is the line between truth and fiction in this genre called "reality" that didn't even exist when we were growing up, but now accounts for 750 of the roughly 1,150 prime-time shows on cable television?

At some point or another, most unscripted shows will come under attack as fake by viewers, tabloids, or Internet trolls, and there are without question cases where the suspicions are justified. Perhaps you've wondered if some cast members on your favorite soapy reality show genuinely do get into physical confrontations with their friends every time they go on vacation or host a dinner party. Or you question whether the aspiring chefs in a popular cooking competition are told before filming ever begins what the challenges will be and what dishes they should prepare. Maybe you're one of the skeptics who assumes we stage the problems for Jonathan to fix in the rundown ramblers I negotiate down to a price our newlywed homebuyers can afford.

No offense taken!

The truth is, anyone who suggests that reality TV doesn't sometimes require readjustments isn't living in the real world—where real weather, real noise, real accidents, and real-life screwups affect what

Like when you split the seat of your pants yet again and have to change?

would otherwise have been our perfect, authentic, real-time shot. Out of those three desirables, real-time is the only one we can't recover once it's lost.

With our shows, the stories are authentic, the homeowners are real, and when the sh*t hits the fan . . . we actually need a cleanup on aisle 3. The big difference is that we're only looking to recapture actual events, not create them out of thin air. In the home-improvement and design subcategory of reality TV, we have a fan base that's interested in learning from the experts as well as watching just for entertainment. Sometimes it's necessary to highlight a particular trouble spot and show how the issue was resolved.

Jonathan and I are executive producers for all our shows. We review every cut and give notes for editing. Sometimes we might find a scene was cut halfway through Jonathan talking about a technical issue, and it comes out meaning the opposite of what he intended. The last thing we want is to send some DIY viewer deep into the remodeling weeds because we left some key step in creating a tray ceiling on the cutting-room floor.

That said, there are big lines that we never cross: Producers don't come to us with a phony "story line" they want us to follow, or dialogue they want the homeowners to memorize. Likewise, if a pipe bursts and floods the basement Jonathan is converting into the cozy in-law suite on the homeowners' wish list, it's not because we sabotaged the plumbing for dramatic effect, LOL. (Pranking Jonathan falls under my personal Brother Exemption, and any damage is strictly psychological, not structural.)

This was our profession long before we had hair-and-makeup calls prior to demolishing an outdated kitchen. Our integrity matters to us not merely for the sake of our TV shows, but for the integrity of who we are as human beings. We truly care about the quality of our work and always put the clients' needs first.

Knowing that we are legitimately helping families get into homes they thought they could never own means a lot to us. There's no way the budgets our families have could translate into the finished dream homes we give them if it weren't for the advantages they score by being cast for *Property Brothers* or *Buying & Selling*. For starters, I don't charge a real estate commission, and they get a free general contractor— Jonathan isn't charging for his time or labor, and if the homeowner's budget suffers unforeseen hits that seriously impact the reno, Jonathan will jump in and take on even more of the labor himself to shave some costs. Another reason why the money our show clients shell out for a reno stretches farther than it would in the non-TV world is because anytime we get wholesale pricing from a vendor, we pass that savings along to the homeowner without markup. Nobody can stretch a budget like we can.

When we do flips, like on *Brother vs. Brother*, we are investing our own money, so we're not necessarily working with homeowners, but we are indeed letting the buyers decide our fate. Because of that, the stress really falls on our shoulders as we try to get these projects done. Some are easier than others, and we've learned the hard way that in this biz you just have to accept the unexpected. Here are some of my "favorite" do-overs, thanks to the gods of Reality Interruptus:

We even pimp ourselves out to get the homeowners as much free stuff as we can.

- While filming a *Property Brothers* scene, my clients, Jonathan, and I were walking up to a house to tour, and a crazy neighbor came running out of her house with a large chef's knife in hand, screaming that we were trying to rob her and she was going to call the police. I could see why she might think Jonathan was some drifter up to no good, but I was standing there in suit and tie. "I must be the best-dressed robber you've ever seen," I politely pointed out. I explained that we were touring the house next door to hers, and she finally calmed down.

- A lot of our homeowners get worked up when it comes to budget, renovations, hand-me-down furniture we want them to get rid of, and so forth. We do trim content that might make them look unlikable. We're notorious for teasing and bantering with our homeowners for a laugh, but it's all in good fun and more often than not, we make ourselves the brunt of a joke. We would never intentionally humiliate anyone for entertainment's sake, and we'll save our homeowners from themselves if we have to. That was the case once on *Buying & Selling*, when our client walked into her house renovation while Jonathan and his crew were working and called everything to a halt with an important announcement: "If my cat walks into the room while you guys are working, you all must stop immediately. No one is allowed to work until my cat decides to leave on its own." She was serious. We removed this from the show because she looked kind of nuts. (But hey, we're keeping it here because it was years ago . . . we've moved on. And cats can't read.)

*Property Mimes,
anyone?*

- While filming in front of a flooring store in Atlanta, this guy on a bicycle zipped by in the middle of the scene, ringing his bell. If we had the person sign a release to be on camera, no problem. But this video-bomber happened to be the R&B artist Usher. Everyone was so star-struck, he was already two blocks away by the time our director thought to ask him if we could keep him in the scene. *Usher, come baaack!* Lesson learned. You can bet we kept our eyes peeled for Blake Shelton on a moped while filming in Nashville.

- Sound is a very important part of any show. If you don't have clean audio, the viewer is going to be distracted. One day, as I was trying to talk with the homeowners, sound issues kept popping up one after another after another. No joke: plane, train, bus, motorbike, MARCHING BAND (*c'mon!*), dogs, baby in stroller, more dogs, the local school letting out. Just when we thought that—at last—all was good, a bird with the most obnoxious wailing cry ever landed in the tree above me.

What makes more sense? Doing a scene chatting with homeowners when a loud train rolling through makes the audio unusable, or re-delivering those lines so audio is clean and the viewer gets the content loud and clear? I don't consider the latter "faking it." Faking it would be if those homeowners were actors pretending to buy and renovate a house. Staging it would be if the cat walked into the room wearing a little hardhat.

Speaking of hardhats and do-overs . . .

Now THAT video would go viral . . .

debonair

Little-known fact: I was originally cast as the contractor on *Property Brothers*, and Jonathan was supposed to be the real estate agent. Both of us had a ton of experience in construction *and* real estate, but the producer thought I looked a little more brawny, and as Jonathan was the broker for our company, they thought he was more the "~~suit~~" guy. The reality was, I wasn't a licensed contractor, nor did I go to college for construction like Jonathan did, and he hadn't been licensed as an agent nearly as long as I had. But we thought this was a great opportunity and didn't want to rock the boat, so didn't challenge them on it. I remember feeling the butterflies in my stomach back when we arrived in Toronto for our first day of filming. We knew our stuff when it came to real estate and renovations—that wasn't worrying me at all. What rattled me was the thought that this could be the gateway to a whole new direction in our lives. All those years of hard work were seemingly about to pay off as our TV and real estate worlds were suddenly colliding. It was kind of like that classic cartoon where the dog finally catches a car after a lifetime chasing them, then sits in the street, mind blown, wondering: *Now what?*

Ever since we were little boys, I've had the sense that we were not your typical kids. We weren't outcasts or, as far as I know, junior aliens exiled from some distant planet that wanted some peace and quiet. But there was no doubt that we marched to the beat of a different drummer, and we generally marched in double-time, changing directions at whim. We were a two-man scramble band, and the half-time show never ended.

While in high school, Jonathan and I made a pact that we would *Just say it loud and say it proud: We're weirdos.*

219

I stand by my theory that my calculations were sound . . . though somehow the Camaro never showed up . . .

become wildly successful one day. Jonathan even wrote himself a post-dated check for a million dollars and carried it around in his wallet along with a picture of the silver Camaro he planned to buy himself once the check had cleared. For the record, Jonathan didn't fully grasp accounting practices at that point. In his mind, the Camaro would be free because it was being "written off" as a business expense. Why didn't more people think of this? We were going to do something special with our lives—we just knew it. And the emphasis was on *doing,* not daydreaming. All the wacky business ventures we got into as kids—starting with those decorative hangers at age 7—had shown us that extra effort always paid off. We couldn't wait to see where hard work and perseverance would eventually take us.

And now, at the age of 32, we were about to find out.

It was just before we arrived at the production offices that I clarified our real estate resumes, and almost immediately they swapped the roles to maintain authenticity. I can safely say that even though I am very competent with the hands-on side of renovations, the show would not have seen the same success without Jonathan in that role. His knowledge as a licensed contractor is deeper than mine, and I still cringe at the thought that I could have been spending every day of the past eight years on a dirty, dusty construction site. Yuck. LOL.

Jonathan was pumped about the Armani suits he expected to find waiting for him in Wardrobe, and was no doubt hoping I'd end up

It's not dust and dirt. It's man glitter.

Good thing I have a perfect match ready on standby if I need transfusions or a new kidney. Whoa. Not so fast, Frankenstein.

dressed in canvas carpenter overalls with a nail apron, or maybe baggy painter's pants. Then, presto change-o, Magic Man, *I'm* the one sorting through my rack of tailored suits and artful array of silk ties while Jonathan can be heard protesting in his deflated-but-brave voice, "But I don't *wear* flannel." I was too busy admiring my Italian leather shoes to hear how he managed to ditch the lumberjack look and feed his plaid-diction instead.

The network couldn't have known this yet, but that last-minute role reversal saved them a fortune in wardrobe replacement and dry cleaning bills . . . because Jonathan has a history of bleeding dramatically. If I cut myself, even deeply, it stops bleeding almost right away. Jonathan can get a paper cut or a ripped hangnail, and he bleeds a loooooong time. We're both sticklers for safety, but there have been some injury situations over the years, so we try not to become complacent.

The scariest incident was Jonathan cutting a second-story window opening from the inside with a reciprocating saw on an episode of *Property Brothers*. He had asked the construction team to make sure everything was clear on the exterior, and they had given him the go-ahead. After cutting across the top, though, the saw got caught on something. Assuming it was just a nail, Jonathan kept going. After about ten seconds, though, something just didn't seem right. He busted a hole in the wall a foot or so to the left and peered out, only to discover that he was about to cut through the house's main power line. For some reason—fear of interrupting a scene, maybe—the contractor watching from the outside hadn't said a word. If Jonathan had cut through, he would be dead. Thereafter, Jonathan implemented a rigorous safety and communication protocol.

I nearly lost it over another close call, this time in Austin. I was showing a house to clients while Jonathan was working on a reno across town. My phone rang: "A beam fell on Jonathan and he's on the way to the hospital!" the producer reported breathlessly. I felt this jolt of pure shock slam me in the chest. Beams can weigh upwards of 1,000 pounds. A horrifying image of my brother crushed beneath flashed through my mind.

"What the hell happened?" I shouted into the phone as I raced for my car. There was no way such a serious accident could have happened if all our safety precautions had been followed. Anger was the only way to push back my fear. Nobody had any answers, and I needed to get to the hospital, fast. My phone rang again just as I was leaving.

"He's okay. It wasn't a beam, it was just a piece of wood that fell from the ceiling and a nail punctured his wrist," I was told. It had hit an artery, and Jonathan the Bleeder had apparently finished his scene like Julia Child on that famous *Saturday Night Live* skit with a butcher knife. Then he blacked out, probably not so much from blood loss as from his body just hitting its limit. He'd been working four months without a day off, and his immune system had already staged a series of protests, including cases of mono and shingles. Being spiked by a rogue nail dropping out of nowhere was merely adding injury to a series of bodily insults. Of course, Jonathan was right back on site as soon as he came to and coagulated.

We had to replace the floor and repaint the blood-spattered wall, though, so the buyers wouldn't suspect we'd flipped a murder house.

Exhaustion is unavoidable when you're filming up to fifty episodes a year across five separate series, a feat possible only because we shoot multiple shows in each location and hire local construction crews, design assistants, and real estate agents to help us. When you add the production crew, caterers, and other folks who help us keep our traveling circus in peak form, we create about 150 local jobs wherever we end up shooting.

In Toronto this fall, for example, we are scheduled to reno seventeen houses during our three-month stay for *Property Brothers* and *Buying & Selling*. That means looking at several houses for sale every day for me, and jumping between multiple construction sites on any given day for Jonathan. Of all those renovations, we can find ourselves actively running up to thirteen at a time. (Yes, we're a well-oiled machine.) Each of the job sites is assigned its own full-time local general contractor as a construction lead—essential not just because of the time crunch, but because they know the local bureaucracy inside out when it comes to pulling permits, scheduling inspections, and dealing with the mountain of paperwork that goes with any building project.

Our biggest priority is making sure the homeowners are taken care of and have a warranty on all the work long after we pull up stakes and leave town. Having local designers work with us, too, speeds up the process of sourcing the best products, whether it's a unique mantel from a salvage yard or custom work from a local artist. And it's fun to keep building such a great network of local friends to pal around with if we pass through town again. That's true with the homeowners, too. There are some we always look up and hang out with when we're back New York, as well as others we worked with in Toronto who come visit us and stay at our house in Las Vegas.

I still laugh when I hear that.

And yes, of the 272 houses we've renovated on-air to date, there are a few that we'll remember even though we're not hanging out and having pajama parties. There was one place featured in *Buying & Selling* where the homeowner carried around this massive angora rabbit that could have doubled as an overstuffed ottoman. Rabbit Lady was married to a guy who seldom spoke while we were around and didn't seem to notice the missus had her flirty ways with me. I smiled through clenched teeth every time she called me "Drewy."

The house was a cluttered maze of chopped-up little rooms with random walls, and the couple's décor was uber-traditional with a splash of dog hair and rabbit droppings. Jonathan proposed knocking down a bunch of walls to give the house some breathing room. We explained as diplomatically as possible that the hoard of kitschy knickknacks and jumble of furniture in every room was not going to attract buyers, but the wife resisted clearing it out and her husband mostly stood by, still saying nothing. We probably should have cut our losses and run for the hills then and there, but thanks to Dad and his sacred Cowboy Code, we felt honor-bound to persevere and finish what we started.

Amazingly, the house turned out to be a small diamond buried deep in the coal mine. With bigger, brighter rooms; clean, modern staging; and no more angora rabbit fur floating off every surface, it promised to sell well. But the whole process was like pulling teeth, and right up until the very end, we couldn't convince Rabbit Lady that her taste was . . . one of a kind.

It happens quite often on *Buying & Selling* when we fix the house in preparation to put it on the market that the homeowners seriously reconsider leaving once they see what we've done. They momentarily forget the reason they wanted to move in the first place: their house

Seriously, remember the homeowner who wanted a cabinet-free kitchen? How does that work, exactly?

didn't have enough bedrooms for their family, or it wasn't in the right school district. They look at that gleaming new kitchen or spa-like bath and try to convince themselves that it could work. This is where I really have to become the mediator for the couple—or a therapist, even. Most assume they're the first homeowners ever experiencing their dilemma, but we've pretty much seen it all.

Besides the occasional wasp nest in the walls, secret possum head-quarters in an attic, or Twilight Zone-y collection of old baby dolls, we find some . . . let's say, unique, items in these houses. While renovating a hoarder's former home, Jonathan opened the walls to discover a vast assortment of stolen road signs used as sheeting instead of plywood. Our most exciting discovery was an unlocked safe hidden under the carpet in a master closet. Inside were some old family photographs and cash. Jonathan and I enjoy solving mysteries and puzzles so we were eager to play detective and track down the proper owner of the found treasure. We were, in fact, able to follow property records and iden-tify the children of the since-deceased homeowner, but the network refused to show the footage of us appearing on her doorstep to give back the safe for fear it would somehow make us look like "plunderers."

We've only ever had to pull the plug once during filming. While we want homeowners to feel we appreciate their situation, we still have to try to encourage them in the right direction for their needs. One homeowner was hearing none of that.

He had been cast because he seemed like the ideal ready-for-

Usually people listen to me when I'm carrying power tools.

Do you think a contractor calendar would outsell a firefighter one?

prime-time candidate: He was a handsome firefighter with quirky taste, and he had all our female colleagues swooning at first sight. Even better, he would be bringing his firefighter buddies along to help him with the labor. Jonathan was finally going to have a run for his money in the slow-mo-reno-in-tight-jeans department.

Like many of the potential buyers who apply to be cast on our shows, the fireman had already done a lot of his own legwork to narrow down the list of homes he was interested in. That's always a plus: We learned the high price of client indecision on our very first episode of *Property Brothers*, which ended up being the most expensive pilot Cineflix had ever shot thanks to the drawn-out agony of our buyers poring over every listing on the market and making me show a ridiculous number of them.

The firefighter hadn't merely narrowed his options, it turned out: He had decided—absolutely—which house he wanted. When we arrived to check it out, we discovered that the place was sinking. *Literally.* The neighborhood was built atop an old landfill that had been converted to residential zoning. The firefighter's dream house had sunk so much on one end that the living room floor felt like a ski slope. The homeowner wanted Jonathan to do a cheap, quick fix, and his idea was to just level out the floor but not do any repair to the structure—completely illegal home "improvements" that would leave the front end of the living room with an 8-foot ceiling but the back corner of the house 18 inches lower.

We warned the buyer that everything we do has to be completely to code, and we would not represent him if he was buying this particular

house. I showed him several better options on the market. He ended up buying the sinking house to renovate on his own, which is a shame, because it was definitely a money pit and he'll never see any value from the investment. The firefighter's fiasco remains the only episode we started to film that never made it to air.

Before everyone with a 1989 kitchen and a firefighter's uniform from last Halloween starts bombarding us with pleas to put their house renos on the show, some full disclosure: We have nothing to do with where we shoot or who gets cast. I'm not kidding... Jonathan and I can't get you to the top of the list. *I swear.* So PLEASE stop sending us bribes/gifts, as they go directly to charity anyway. (Except the disturbing ones that go straight to a faraway Dumpster or to the proper authorities. We mean *you*, weird artisanal soap-maker who mailed us a bar containing locks of your hair and lingerie. And *you*, suspicious distributor of gold bars who sent us an unsolicited brick in hopes we could be bought. And *especially you*, creepy person who cut the heads off people in a series of family portraits like a serial killer and pasted ours in their place.)

The network and the production company choose a location based on diversity of architecture and the homeowner demographic. Also taken into consideration are the logistics of getting us to and from a major airport, since a lot of our down time away from set is spent traveling for appearances or press. There also has to be easy access to a pool of skilled local workers and supplies. We pushed for two years to film in Nashville before the network execs finally caved and agreed. Without being bribed.

We get thousands of applications to be featured on the show, but most are from people who have no budget and no intention of buying

First time if they so much as mention homemade soap.

or selling—they just want a free house. (Unfortunately, that's not how it works.) Then there are the ones who simply harbor a mad crush on one or both of us, but they're quickly weeded out by the fifth time they ask how soon until they meet us in person. None of the nudist families who've applied have made it on yet, but we have had couples move up their wedding to be married on the show, and even one pair who offered to induce early for a delivery of twins during filming. It's amazing how competitive people can be for the opportunity. You don't have to be a married couple to get on the show, but if you're single, you need to have a likeable sidekick such as a best friend or relative so there's someone to discuss your decisions with. We don't have an inter-cranial camera capable of filming you talking to yourself inside your head.

We're pumped to have such a big international viewership, even if we can't translate tweets into Flemish or Croatian. We get people as far away as Dubai applying to be on the show, but when we've got 17 projects on the go, it would be hard for 16 to be in Connecticut and one in the Middle East. Or Brazil, which probably has our most enthusiastic fan base.

Three months before we set up shop in our next location, we send a team to start looking for real estate, construction, and production professionals who really love doing what they do and can do it well enough to meet our high expectations. If we aren't already familiar with one of our upcoming locations, Jonathan and I make a trip, too, just to explore and get a sense of the vibe.

YET! Patent pending . . .

WE ALWAYS TELL CLIENTS,
TRADES, AND ANYBODY WORKING
ON THE SHOWS THAT IT'S
GOING TO BE CRAZY,
STRESSFUL AT TIMES, A TON
OF WORK-BUT SO WORTH IT
IN THE END. THEY JUST HAVE
TO TRUST US :)
-Drew

Or in the middle of one of your stories.

Nashville was high on our wish list because we're crazy about the city and not-so-secretly wanted to be able to meet up with friends in the country music industry and do a little house-hunting of our own when we could break away from filming for a few hours. We've hosted the main stage for the CMA music festival five years running, and Nashville feels like a home-away-from-home to us already.

More often than not, though, when we have a rare day off from filming the two shows, we end up flying to another city to do press, film commercials, attend events, make scheduled appearances, or work on other business ventures. It's a good thing the ability to fall instantly asleep is our superpower, because we spend a lot of time on red-eye flights. Jonathan could seriously even fall asleep in an active rock quarry.

Being in demand is any celebrity's wish fulfilled, and it's amazing to go from being Doublemint Twin rejects to turning down offers to appear on a dozen shows because we don't have the time, or it's not a good fit. Before snagging Jacinta's heart, Jonathan may have been longing to find love, but he's allergic to drama and manipulation, so accepting an invitation to become *The Bachelor* was a non-starter. *The Amazing Race* would be . . . well . . . amazing, but I think I'd stand a better chance of winning if I teamed up with Linda. Jonathan and I did do a cooking competition in Canada once called *Extreme Potluck*, which I, of course, won, and Jonathan predictably lost—big-time.

The challenge was to prepare a meal with the theme of Canadian cuisine for fifty unknown judges. We assumed because it was in a rural setting and they were "local area experts" that the judges would

You take that back!

234

Nobody in the history of the world has ever said "I'm going to win with meatloaf."

likely be farmers. Celebrities were paired up randomly and tasked with creating a winning dish. My teammate wanted to make her famous meatloaf, and I prepared Linda's family recipe for roasted butternut squash with cinnamon and crushed almonds.

Jonathan made Canadian beef tenderloin with garlic mashed potatoes. His steak was so dry and overdone, it stood a better chance of winning the Stanley Cup as a hockey puck.

The coolest thing about becoming the Property Brothers hasn't been the fame, but the familiarity. People feel like they really do know us and treat us like we're part of the family. We have fans pull up a chair and share their stories if they spot us in a local restaurant. They see us shopping at home improvement stores and try like friendly border collies to herd us into the paint section in hopes we'll end their chip-anxiety. They try to set us up with daughters, granddaughters, nieces, and neighbors. By the millions they keep inviting us into their homes on a daily basis. They laugh with us and at us, and we'll take either.

We just want to keep it real.

Not my fault! We cooked it perfectly, but when the show transported our food to location, they left the warmers on high. Grrr.

BRO VS. BRO

Jonathan

The reveal is always such a great moment on every show we do, and I never get tired of seeing the astonishment on the homeowners' faces when they see their transformed home. That we're able to keep it a surprise is a pretty amazing accomplishment, too, considering what a blabbermouth Drew is.

Drew cannot be trusted with secrets.

One couple we were working with had just discovered they were expecting a baby, but it was still early and they were keeping the exciting news under wraps.

We threw a party for the episode's reveal, and all of the homeowners' family and friends had flown in for it. The couple stressed that none of us, under any circumstances, should breathe a word about the pregnancy. Everybody on the crew knew that mum was the word.

There were about fifty people at the party. I gave a speech about how wonderful our clients had been and what a great episode this would be.

Then Drew stepped out in front of everybody, put his hand on the wife's belly and said, "AND, this beautiful space isn't the ONLY surprise—"

The homeowner froze, her eyes like saucers. Our director was giving Drew the "shush" face. Too late. The family was going nuts with joy.

Drew swore that we told him everybody knew, and that's probably what he heard, because he doesn't pay attention.

Drew

Jonathan has a tendency to embellish stories. Of course, *I* never would, because I'm the trustworthy one. On that *Property Brothers* episode, I knew that the homeowner was going to make the pregnancy announcement a part of the show. We were having a big wrap-party with all of her family and our crew.

"Has she told everyone?" I asked someone on our crew, wanting to make sure, before I said anything, that the coast was clear.

"Everyone knows." But he thought I was only referring to the crew.

During the party, the homeowner gave a beautiful speech, saying, "This is truly our dream home. We couldn't have done it without Jonathan and Drew." Jonathan tacked on how fun they were to work with and how thrilled we were to be able to surprise them with their new space. She then handed the mic to me. I had a beautiful and touching speech of my own planned, starting with placing my hand on her stomach and saying, "The house wasn't the only surprise—"

Right away, I heard a collective gasp from our crew, who were all lined up to my side. They were all frantically dragging their fingers across their throats to signal me to cut. I realized to my horror that I had been misinformed, but there was no going back. The homeowner awkwardly made the best of the situation and confirmed she was expecting.

"Well, I was going to wait to tell you until the show aired," she told her family, "but . . . Surprise! I'm pregnant!"

Before we get to the confidentiality faux pas, I'd like to just point out that I not only can keep a secret, but I can orchestrate and carry out a stealth plan with 007 confidence and cool. Anybody remember my crazy proposal to Linda that was months in the making, involving secret email accounts, burner phones, hidden cameras, and trays of diamonds? Exactly! She had no clue.

WE EACH HAVE THE
CHOICE WHETHER TO
BE A GOOD OR A BAD
INFLUENCE IN THE
LIVES OF OTHERS.
                    -Jonathan

JONATHAN

Comments by Drew

SPEAK UP, STEP UP

We were coming back from an amusement park called Playland when it happened. Two men, loud and drunk, boarded the bus. They were covered in dirt, and their ankles were spattered with blood. One of them carried a scythe. I don't remember how old Drew and I were, exactly, but we had to be in our early teens. We watched nervously as the drunks lurched down the aisle, menacing our fellow passengers along the way.

They sexually harassed some young women with vulgar comments and lewd gestures before targeting the ethnic minorities with racial slurs and homophobic taunts. I remember the scythe-wielder turning back to Drew and me for validation and encouragement—"Right? Isn't that right?"—as he lit into a black gentleman, assuming we shared his hatred because we were white, too. It was sickening. Drew and I just sat there frozen. Neither of us said anything. Everybody on the bus was just sitting there taking it, afraid to provoke the bullies more, all of us no doubt hoping that silently looking out the windows would spare us from becoming their next victim.

Suddenly the bus driver slammed on the brakes, causing the drunks to stumble to their knees. The driver jumped out of his seat and stormed down the aisle. "Enough!" he roared as he physically shoved the two thugs out the door and onto the pavement.

The bus erupted in cheers and clapping.

Instead of basking in his moment of heroic glory, the driver then turned on the lot of us with undisguised disgust.

"No!" he shouted. "No! You should all be ashamed of yourselves. You sat here for five minutes and didn't say a word while people were being berated and harassed. You shouldn't be applauding me, you should be ashamed of yourselves."

He was right.

I remember vowing to myself right then and there: *I will never sit and be quiet again.*

I knew without even asking that Drew was thinking the same. We both knew better. We'd been raised to always help someone in need, to stand up not only for ourselves and for each other, but for anyone being treated badly. We'd done this so many times before at school or

It made me feel that even though I was a kid, I should never be afraid to stand up for what's right.

on the playground, but this ride was the first time we'd been in a situation involving adults, and we were scared. Not to mention confused when the adults didn't step up. What we learned on that pivotal afternoon was to not ever stand on protocol or wait to take our cue from anyone else if we knew what was happening was wrong. It didn't matter whether we were 15 years old or 50: Moral responsibility doesn't carry a "best if used by" label.

We didn't even make it through the first day of high school without becoming a bully's prime target. Drew and I were laughing and goofing around in the hallway. Drew grabbed one of my books and darted away from me just as this older kid was coming around the corner, and they slammed into each other. No damage, no injuries, no problem. Yeah right. The guy's angry red face and instant death threat indicated that a hasty apology wasn't going to suffice, no matter how sincere. He spent the rest of the semester trying to catch Drew so he could pulverize him, but the doppelganger advantage confused him no end. Just to cover his bases, he'd stop whichever one of us he saw first.

"Are you the one, or are you the other one?" he would demand.

"I'm Jonathan, you want Drew," I would respond. Drew would do the same if he got cornered. The bully would then demand to know which way Drew went and would be sent tearing off in another direction. And if for some reason he'd encounter the other one of us en route, we already had a plan for that, too.

"Hey! Where are you going? I just told you Drew went *that* way!"

It was like we were directing and starring in our own cartoon.

By the following year, Drew and I were starting to enjoy a little taste of popularity—funny and athletic made up some for skinny and nerdy, and my magic came in handy, too. (Levitating is a great party trick.) Fitting in and maybe even being considered cool wasn't a goal, but I won't lie and say it wasn't welcome. Pedro, Drew, and I were notorious for pulling pranks and doing what amounted to a running improv-comedy routine that still hasn't broken for intermission 25 years later.

We all get caught up sometimes in what starts out as a joke or gag but somehow ends up crossing a line to become insensitive—or just plain mean. My moment of clarity came in ninth grade. I was messing around, teasing this one unpopular kid, just trying to be funny when, without even thinking about it, I reached over, gave him a jab, and knocked a book out of his hand. It ate me up over the coming weeks and made for many sleepless nights. I tried to make it up to him by being inclusive for the rest of our high school years, but why didn't I just do that in the first place?

The whole not-brave new world of social media has made it far easier for people who are not inherently unkind to become vicious, egged on by the competitive cruelty of Internet trolls who entertain each other by seeing who can come up with the most hurtful put-down in some mob attack on a public forum. That old saying about "words can never hurt me" has never been less true than it is today—just look at the number of teen suicides that have been linked to cyber-bullying in recent years. Even one is too many.

As TV personalities who enjoy interacting with fans through social media, we're very aware of what's on our different platforms at any given time. We're hands-on, whether it's Facebook, Instagram, Twitter, Snapchat, etc. Drew could get sucked into the Bermuda Triangle and

Mainly I ignore them. There's nothing I could say or do that would make them feel better.

he'd still be posting pumped-up workout videos or clever little jabs at me. Do we get haters posting rude comments about us? Sure, but ignoring negative attention-seekers is the best way to silence them. There's no point in feeding them or cleaning up after them.

At least, that's what I always told myself.

Until January 21, 2017.

Equal rights is a cause we have always embraced, and if we hadn't been filming, Drew and I would have gone with Jacinta, Linda, and JD's girlfriend, Annalee, to join the Women's March on Washington. More than a million people turned out around the globe to stand up in support of women's rights. I posted a vintage black-and-white photo of a women's march from 50-plus years ago—a reminder of how maddeningly slow progress is—along with a caption that read: "They are our sisters, our mothers, our daughters, our partners, and our friends. They are strong, intelligent, courageous women who deserve to be heard. A culture that respects & supports its women is one destined for great things."

Along with the thumbs-up, hearts, and inspiring messages came the predictable backlash—not only from the usual trolls, but from some particularly vile ranks of people who seem to consider entitlement a political party and contempt their religion.

Every now and then, I'll do a rant post concerning human rights or injustice. I try not to stoop to the level of the enemy. I've learned that if you make the effort to rant eloquently instead of incoherently, anyone taking offense is just going to look dim.

About to head for dinner in Vegas with the family, I snagged Drew and asked him to film a quick video. He hit record, and I spoke from the heart for 1 minute, 37 seconds:

Think back to when you were a child and your parents taught you that if you don't have something nice to say, don't say anything at all. I have no idea what happened to that. Because I read all of your posts. And fortunately, most of our fans are incredible and they have insightful comments, and I love sharing their stories and that's great.

But we also have some people who are just cruel and angry, and no matter what, they just have something negative to say. This is not the place for that. Not to mention that we have a lot of kids who read these posts actively . . .

If it offends you when I post saying I believe in human rights or I believe in equality or even just simple human kindness, then I think you need to take a good look in the mirror and find your source of unhappiness.

When you choose to look at the world from a place of hostility, well, it's unlikely you're going to see even the smallest amount of good. And that is a tragedy . . .

And when I see this inspiring situation where strangers have come together all over the world to express their peaceful passions for justice, well, that has resonated to areas on the planet where unfortunately people don't experience the same democratic freedoms that we have. But someday I hope that they will.

I just believe that any achievement for equality here in America is a victory for human rights around the world. Period.

The rant went viral. Before I knew it, the video had drawn a reach of 1.4 million views, 42,000 reactions, and 6,000 comments on my Facebook page. It was picked up by hundreds of magazines, newspapers,

It would be shock therapy if Fitbits counted the number of negative things we say or do along with the number of steps we take each day. . . .

entertainment shows, and local news programs. Apparently, I struck a nerve, and I'm glad.

I could only hope my plea to be kind and civilized would resonate with those who needed to hear it most—the ones who knew better, but were still sitting silently on that bus while others on the same journey were in peril.

Sometimes I think people just don't notice that they're no longer passing quickly through negative space, but in fact are renting to own. When do sarcastic jokes reach the tipping point and turn into nothing but a steady drip of criticisms? Avoiding someone who's shape-shifted into a spitting viper is understandable. Not shouting a warning first in case they hadn't noticed is unforgiveable. I remember going on a date with an influential actress who had a public image built around being charming and entrepreneurial. She was hugely successful and had far more fans and followers than I did; people genuinely admired her. I was looking forward to getting to know her. We went to dinner at a nice restaurant, and she immediately started making all these mean little observations about the diners surrounding us.

"Look at that hideous outfit she's wearing," or "Can you believe he'd go out in public with a face like that?"

Every time I tried to steer her into anything resembling an actual grown-up conversation, she would go right back to her insult monologue. It was supposed to be witty and droll, I guess, but it definitely wasn't attractive.

Finally I just put it out there: "Look, I feel this may not be working. You're pretty focused on criticizing everyone, and I'm not into that kind of negativity." She was highly offended, called me an asshole, and stormed off. Six months later, I was shocked when I received a text from her out of the blue that said "Thank you." No one had ever dared to call her out on it before. She admitted that she wasn't raised like that, nor did she want that to be what defined her. It was reassuring to hear.

The gift of celebrity comes, I believe, with a social contract. Jennifer Lawrence put it best when she said: "What's the point in having a voice at all if I'm not going to use it for what I truly believe in?"

To those online who say we should stick to renovating houses and stop giving opinions on anything else, I say shame on you. Shame on you for suggesting that one's profession defines who they are as a human or what they truly believe in. Shame on you for closing your mind to a point of view different from your own. Humanity has evolved by learning from the errors of our past and struggling to improve for the future. Change is as frightening as it is inevitable.

When we were kids and fantasizing the way kids do about becoming rich and famous someday, our mom would temper our ambition with compassion, reminding us, "You don't need a million dollars to make a difference."

Our parents supported many different causes both locally and abroad, and we learned the value of giving back through the example they set. Our home, nestled in nature, and their love of the Rocky Mountains taught us to treat the land with reverence, and made us mindful of the marks we leave on an environment whose gifts are intended to benefit everyone, not just a privileged few.

When we went to install solar panels on our house in Vegas, I soon found myself thrust deep into the trenches of the hot-topic issue of renewable energy, and the David vs. Goliath battle between everyday

I'VE LEARNED THAT IF YOU WANT TO
"DISH IT," YOU GOTTA "TAKE IT."
IF YOU FEEL THE NEED TO RANT, THEN
SOMETIMES YOU ALSO NEED TO LISTEN.
EVERYTHING COMES DOWN TO BALANCE.

-Jonathan

consumers wanting to harness the power of Nevada's abundant sunlight and the powerful few who had a vested interest in thwarting them.

The controversy sparked a fire in me both creatively and politically. I have always believed in having an educated opinion if you're going to stand for something, so I started digging. What I uncovered was frightening. The bully in this case was big business. The victim, all of us. I wrote a documentary on the findings, which exposes corruption, deceit, manipulation, and good old-fashioned greed. The facts are like something straight out of a Hollywood script. But this is all real . . . and it's scary.

I hadn't even finished writing the initial outline when somehow word got out about the project, and I received my first two warnings from some large, influential corporations threatening to blacklist me from working with any of their companies if I continued.

I'm still producing the film.

We were taught at an early age that we could make a big difference in this world, even if it was just a big difference for one other person. There was no minimum age required for a random act of kindness, or taking care of the planet we all share.

There used to be a public basketball court at a park in Maple Ridge where we played every weekend and through much of the summer. One day we showed up to discover that someone had broken the rim right off the backboard, and we could no longer play. They weren't the best backboards and hoops to start with, and even though Parks and Rec was supposed to fix it, when we brought it to their attention, they said they didn't have the budget for repairs. They told us there was no guarantee they would decide to allot the money for the fix in the following year's budget, either.

Drew had run basketball camps for kids, and he understood on a personal level how important the game was as an outlet, especially for many kids who had nowhere else to go. He knew they would be let down by the loss of their practice court. Rather than wait for Parks and Rec to do the right thing, or expend energy mounting a protest that might well prove futile, he saw an opportunity to do something rather than just say something. He may have only been 15, but that didn't stop him from launching his own fundraiser, which ended up raising enough for two brand new backboards and hoops, new lines painted on the court, and a small playground. Even I was blown away by how the whole neighborhood came together to offer their support.

It was also while we were in our teens that we discovered how tender the human bond can be, even between strangers, and how easy it is to acknowledge that connection. Mom and Dad raised us to understand the importance of giving back. When we signed up as volunteers to visit with the young patients in the children's oncology ward of the local hospital, it just seemed like a natural extension of the clown and magic acts we'd been putting on for years at birthday parties. But spending time with children who are in the last few months or weeks of their lives changes you. This wasn't about performing or entertaining someone, really, it was about being there with them. Sharing space that has been stripped bare of ego or expectation, where there's no room left for pretense.

Drew remembers building a birdhouse from a craft-store kit with a boy who had lost his eyesight to cancer, and how excited the little boy was as he felt each piece and Drew guided him by touch through the project. With another child, listening was the greatest gift he could

Kids just want to be kids, to laugh and play and not think about the sickness.

251

IT'S IMPORTANT TO
REALLY THINK ABOUT
WHAT MATTERS TO YOU.
WHAT MOVES YOU. IF
IT'S PEOPLE, ANIMALS,
THE PLANET, OR EVEN
EDUCATION . . . THERE
ARE A MILLION WAYS
TO PITCH IN.

-Jonathan

offer as she confided in him that she was worried about her mother, who had a rough night. "She was crying," the girl told Drew. "I was holding her hand." Drew attended the girl's funeral not long after. To this day he draws inspiration from her courage and compassion even as she faced death at the innocent age of 8.

She didn't have a million dollars, but there is no question that she had an impact. She made a difference to us. All the kids we've met at various hospitals over the years have had an impact on us. The chain reaction of a few hours with one blind boy and birdhouse becomes a lifetime commitment to supporting kids' cancer initiatives for the two teen volunteers who happen to become adult celebrities, who are lucky enough to grow a big fan base whose numbers include many who will step up and do what they can, too.

We don't have the luxury of a lot of down time with our schedules today, but we do have a lot of equity in our brand, and investing that in causes dear to our hearts is as important to us as the checks we write to the charities we support.

Social media has profoundly changed the landscape for raising funds and awareness—just look at the deserving people who have been helped thanks to crowdfunding, or by the research and development of drugs to treat Lou Gehrig's disease thanks to the $115 million raised by the much-ridiculed ice bucket challenge that took the Internet by storm in 2014. We were among the hundreds of celebrities who joined in—it was exciting to be part of such a huge chain reaction for good.

In recent years, we've been able to help raise millions for charities such as Artists for Peace and Justice, World Vision, St. Jude Children's

It originally seemed like a bizarre idea, but ended up starting a conversation, which is the most important thing.

Research Hospital, Rebuilding Together, and Habitat for Humanity. The flip side of having that kind of visibility, though, is having to keep our passion in check sometimes when there's a situation where we feel compelled to step up, but at the same time are constrained by the risks and reservations that come with being in the public eye.

To understand how we "really" are, let's rewind to a high school assembly where the guest speaker was a girl whose twin sister had been killed by a drunk driver in a horrific accident. As she was telling her story, some "cool kid" idiots behind us started laughing and heckling her. Drew grew more and more livid with each jeer, until he was literally shaking with anger. He turned on the leader and grabbed him by the shirt.

"Open your mouth one more time and you're not going to like what happens," he warned. The hecklers could see in Drew's eyes that he wasn't kidding. They shut up.

Then there was me at the age of 23, just another straphanger on a crowded train. A tiny older gentleman, maybe 5 feet tall, was facing me. The train was bouncing him around and he kept accidentally jostling a brick house of a guy behind him. The guy turned around and snarled at him: "Hey, stop bumping me or I'm going to knock you out." The old man apologized. He was trying his hardest not to touch the other passenger, but then the train lurched to another stop, and he bumped the hothead again. I could see the look of sheer terror cross his face as the guy turned on him. "I f---ing warned you . . ." he barked as he lunged toward the elderly man. Before he could finish or take a swing, the doors opened and . . . let's just say I "briskly escorted" him off. "You come back on this train and I'll knock *you* out," I promised.

Thanks to our years studying the discipline of karate, both Drew and I know how to avoid a fight—and how to resolve one quickly with force if necessary. I'm not one to start a fight, but I admit there's a part of me that enjoys it once I'm in one, because you'd better believe the person has it coming if I got pushed that far. It's a hot button for both of us when people are being attacked unfairly.

I felt that button being pushed in a strange bar one night last year in Fargo, North Dakota, after wrapping up a local appearance and going to grab a drink with a friend and some folks I had just met at the event. The first bar was a lot of fun, and the staff even asked me behind the bar to take pictures and show off my wannabe bartending moves. When that bartender was getting off his shift, he suggested we go to this other bar where there was live music. As soon as we entered the second place, I could feel this weird tension between our group and the staff. This continued to brew under the surface for a good hour—when suddenly all the lights went up and they started clearing everybody out. It was closing time. A guy who'd been behind the bar immediately approached our table and was specifically eyeing the couple across from me.

"Get the f--k out, lights up!" he barked.

"What? We literally just ordered our drinks!" someone in our group said. No one had said last call. Something definitely seemed off, and for whatever reason, this couple was being targeted. The bar guy confirmed my hunch.

"Too bad," he said, slapping a drink off the table and sending it smashing to the floor. I didn't know these people, I had no idea what was going on, but this aggression was totally unwarranted.

"Whoa, whoa," I said. "I think we all need to take a breath."

The employee then grabbed the women in our group and began

shoving them out the front while someone else started shoving the guys out the back into an alley. I was still trying to wrap my brain around what was happening and on what planet this kind of treatment was acceptable. The bar was still full of people who were slowly making their way to the exits. My friend was out front by herself, and so I planned to cross back through the bar to get to her. I turned around and took about five steps back inside when one of the bar staff grabbed me by the throat in a chokehold. I didn't struggle, but I couldn't breathe. Never in my life had I been put in a chokehold or thrown out of a bar, let alone for not doing anything. It took everything in me not to revert back to my martial arts training and flip the guy onto his butt. But that wouldn't help the situation. There was something else going on. For all I knew, it could be more than just a beef with these people I had met . . . the whole thing could be a set-up and they were trying to get me to make a scene. Wasn't going to happen.

Back outside, I flagged a passing cop and filed an assault report against the guy who'd practically crushed my windpipe and a complaint against the bar. The officer told me that this was a common complaint police received about this place. When he went back for the video from the security camera, apparently he was told the cameras weren't running that night. Footage miraculously showed up three days later, though—a brief snippet zeroing in on me being hustled toward the back door. By then, tabloid headlines had already circulated saying I was in a bar fight with headlines like "Property Brother Gets His Face Renovated." Granted, I'll give that writer the headline of the year award because that's pretty funny. But the experience as a whole

I woke up to see this headline on my phone. My tactic to avoid any further issues . . . was to promptly go back to sleep.

was anything but funny. I was shaken up, mistreated, and frankly pissed about the whole thing.

Great! That's what you get for standing up for a stranger, I thought to myself. I guess the entire ordeal qualified as first (and only) Property Brothers scandal. Nothing more ever came of the incident, though my friends still make fun of me for my starring role in the lamest reported bar brawl in history, since not a single punch was thrown.

But let's keep some perspective: Nothing could possibly be pettier than first-world problems like celebrity gossip, bar non-brawls, and concerns that some scam artist might stage something so they can shake you down with threats of a lawsuit. I know my place on this vast and troubled planet is nowhere remotely near center stage. Fame isn't power; it's energy. And what that energy can—and should—do is pull attention to the people and places and problems that need it the most.

One of the most humbling experiences I've had in my life was a trip Drew, JD, and I made to India with the humanitarian aid organization World Vision in an attempt to raise awareness about child trafficking and child labor. The slums of New Delhi were a culture shock. Poverty like that doesn't exist in North America. Yet people would be singing while they made their naan, without knowing where their next drink of water or meal was coming from.

At the education centers World Vision set up in the slums, we were each assigned a child to get to know. The little girl we met used to sell trinkets—necklaces she made from flowers and grass—on the roadside to support her family. It was either this or rag picking, scouring the dump barefoot for bits of wood or metal to sell for pennies. In many of these slums, the children work because the parents are unwilling to. It's hard to wrap my brain around the lack of value placed on human life in the eyes of some people. At 7, the girl we befriended had been kidnapped off the street, brutally raped, and then dumped back on the side of the road, barely clinging to life. When her parents got to the hospital, we learned, her father had immediately berated her, demanding to know if she had the money from her flower trinkets.

One of the World Vision representatives told us about another child, around 4, who wasn't her usual carefree self one day when she came to the center. She lifted her tattered shirt to show severe burns on her stomach. A pot of boiling water had fallen on her. The worker went to her parents and asked if the girl had seen a doctor. "I don't know, ask her," was the mother's reply. She was too busy dealing drugs to worry about her own child. Kids as young as 5 and 6 would come to the education centers, blitzed out of their minds because the mothers or fathers decided to silence them by giving them drugs instead of parenting. It was incredibly upsetting to hear their stories and witness their tragedies. But even more heartbreaking was the absence of hope in the eyes of children who'd simply given up on themselves.

No amount of money is going to solve the problem. Support and education are key. People oppressed by slumlords will never rise up and stand up for themselves unless the rest of us show that we're not giving up on them. Maybe it's not the biggest thing in the world, after all, when our grande latte comes with the wrong spice on top. Throw a fit, by all means. But throw it over something you want to see changed in the world, not your coffee. A million voices can make a bigger statement than a million dollars.

Back at home, we're excited when we can use our shows as a gateway to a better life for people who need a hand, or as a way to contribute something to the communities that host us. All the profits from the sales of the homes on *Brother vs. Brother* are donated to charity. Each year, that's meant between $80,000 and $160,000 going to Rebuilding Together, which has put the money right back into the local community. Some of those funds were used to improve a transitional education center that helps people with disabilities learn meaningful skills that will help them find employment. Another year, the money renovated and improved a Boys & Girls Club facility. This year, we also donated over $250,000 in new furniture and decor from Wayfair to the Habitat for Humanity ReStore. We can't stress enough that every little bit counts. One dollar. One tweet. One hour helping out at your local food bank or animal shelter. It matters.

The holidays are especially rough for many families who have fallen on hard times, so every year we try to give some folks the Christmas they thought they'd never have. Most of these people never expected to be in such a place and had no control over what forced them there. I remember that feeling of failure and shame when I had to declare bankruptcy in my 20s. It's very hard to ask for help when you've never had to ask before. But we all need a little help at some point in our lives—when we've reached the end of our rope and all we can do is tie a knot and hang on.

In New Orleans, we found an amazing charitable organization called SBP that was trying to help families affected by Hurricane Katrina, who are still struggling to get on their feet more than a decade later. SBP raises money for renovations to make homes livable again. We partnered with them to shoot a special *Brothers Take New Orleans* series to renovate a duplex that had been uninhabitable from the water and wind damage Katrina caused in August 2005.

The duplex belonged to a woman who had put every dime she had

Hearing this nearly brought tears to my eyes. I want everyone to feel they DO deserve a beautiful place to live and that there is hope in all aspects of their lives.

into fixing the damage to her home, only to have the contractor she hired rip the house apart and take off with the money. For the past 11 years, she had been living on a mattress on the floor of a rental apartment 45 minutes out of town. Even working three jobs, that's all she could afford. The natural disaster had taken everything else from her.

We came in and fully renovated the duplex from top to bottom, complete with brand-new furniture and decor. When the owner came to see the progress on her house, she didn't understand why we would be doing something like this for her. She said she didn't deserve it.

When the project was done, the woman moved back in and was so incredibly thankful. I can't imagine being forced out of my home, not to return for 11 years. She let her brother's family move into the other side of the duplex, which was a wonderful gesture and showed she was already paying it forward.

There's nothing we cherish more than family, and the strength we draw from our own clan inspires us every single day. When Dad had a health scare last year, we thought we were going to lose him. He was 82, and a kidney infection became so serious, he dropped 50 pounds and landed in the ICU. The doctors told Mom to start making final arrangements. None of us were nearby at the time, and she was alone at the hospital with him until we could arrange flights and get there. I remember his voice sounding so weak, we could barely hear him. We learned there was a new kind of surgery that offered a slim hope of saving him, and Dad pulled through. He's regained most of the weight and all of his spirit. That Cowboy Code came through again. *Always finish what you start.*

There's a part of the code I never did really get as a kid but I understand it now: *Always ride for the brand.* It has to do with representing what you stand for, and staying true to it. Our brand is our name, our identity, our family.

It's rare for Drew and I to have a heart-to-heart conversation about the smaller picture instead of the bigger one. When we do talk about what we want our own lives to look like in the near future, we both paint idyllic pictures of marrying our soulmates and designing separate homes with doors that are always open and Monopoly boards always waiting for the ultimate winner-take-all showdown. There'll be kids, of course. Plenty of them, we hope, full of curiosity and confidence and kindness. Twins would be good.

We fantasize about renovating a castle in Scotland someday, or checking off the same wish we both have on our bucket lists—to search for buried treasure. Maybe that sounds childish. I hope so, because growing up shouldn't cost any of us childhood's greatest gifts. That boundless enthusiasm, unbridled imagination, and naive belief that anything is possible is what got us this far, after all. We carry with us the wisdom of cowboys we have known, the mischief of clowns, the discipline of senseis, the mystery of illusionists.

In the end, it's not the stories we tell that matter, but the stories we live. Not just our own, but those we pass through on our way to all those places we still hope to go.

What we don't know is more thrilling than what we already do. We're reminded of this every time we stand in front of yet another door of another house, of another adventure just waiting to be seized.

You can never know what you might find until you get inside.

THE END.

AFTERPARTY

So . . . this is the spot where we're supposed to wrap everything up and say the story's over. Nothing more to see here, please exit in an orderly fashion and take your belongings with you, there are editors waiting to turn out the lights and go home to their own families.

STOP!!! Wait, don't go!!!

Our story's NOT over, and neither is this party. We have plenty of snacks left . . . good ones! There are still cashews in the nut mix. Please help yourselves to this buffet of random stories, weird facts, and embarrassing secrets (like which one of us wears a garter belt).

UH, NO . . . BUT THANKS FOR PLAYING: SHOW TITLES WE REJECTED

When we were originally pitched the idea of doing a show about our real estate business, it had a working title of *My Dream Home*. We felt we could do MUCH better. Here's the actual list of names that came out of our creative session . . . before we eventually wound up agreeing on *Property Brothers*.

What is this, a soap opera?

Sounds familiar . . .

Double Vision	It Takes Two
Home Team	Relative Reno
The Brotherly Way	Scott Free
Our Vision, Your Dreams	Two Men and a Hammer
Mending Fences	Bros Before Renos
Two for the Price of One	Twice as Nice
Bungalow Brothers	Twin Takeover
Mirror Image	Two Ugly Dudes with a Reno to Do
La Casa Nostra	

Yes, we did have that on the list. Ha ha.

CLOWN SCHOOL, CUM LAUDE

We'll bet you didn't know that the best balls for juggling are fuzzy tennis balls sliced open a tiny bit and filled with a small amount of split peas, then taped up again. Only split peas. No black-eyed, chick, or pigeon peas. No idea why. A weight thing? Less likely to jam the vacuum cleaner when the tape comes off midair? Our six-plus years as professionals in the clowning arts taught us this, among many other things that proved never to come in handy when trying to impress the opposite sex. For example, when applying the classic white clown makeup you need to pat the whole face thoroughly, which smooths out the lines, makes you less creepy, and prevents you from looking like you belong in a child's nightmares. And also, the cost-effective secret to locking in that facial makeup freshness . . . baby powder. When it's not being used to prevent diaper rash, it's preserving red noses, fake freckles, and all things clowny.

DOUBLE DARE

In which we name three outrageous dares the other would never accept, and three he probably would . . .

Jonathan

1. Drew would never turn off his phone and give it up. Not for a week, a day, or even an hour. It may actually be his lifeline.

2. He definitely would never roll in insulation—he HATES insulation, and by the way he reacts when I toss it at him, I'm assuming a roll of the stuff either beat him up as a kid or cut him off in traffic.

3. Finally, if I dared Drew to take everything in his overly organized closet and mess it all up for a week, he'd probably have a complete meltdown. There are not many things in this life that stress him out more than lack of organization.

As far as outrageous things I could get him to do on a dare: Hmm . . .

1. Waterfall kayaking. Any extreme sport, really. It's like he has to prove he's fearless.

2. He would also willingly walk up to any complete stranger and convince them to do anything—burp the alphabet, drink one of his disgusting protein shakes . . .

3. . . . and if I dared him to take lessons in anything bizarre, he'd sign right up, if he wasn't already registered. With Drew's competitive spirit, obsession with taking lessons, and drive to succeed, I could probably have him ready for the synchronized swim team by the next Summer Olympics.

Drew

This is a little tricky for Jonathan because he has a lot lower standards than I do.

1. I couldn't dare him to eat a random insect because he'd probably do it, but I BET he wouldn't drink an entire serving of one of my protein shakes, as he finds them absolutely revolting.

2. He also would never do a toothbrush commercial—the sound of a manual toothbrush makes his skin crawl. It's really weird.

3. Lastly, I'd say if I dared him to take a selfie every day for a month, he'd likely disown me as a brother or destroy my phone in protest. He has made it pretty clear that that isn't his thing.

Now for dares he would do . . .

1. Skydiving. He's always wanted to do it. Maybe it's from watching Copperfield fly, but easily that would be a "yes" for Jonathan—except our host insurance policies forbid it.

2. Secondly, go on a survivalist excursion, like *Survivorman* (as long as there was a decent marinade for the grilled scorpions). Jonathan loves to travel more than anybody I know, and he doesn't have to stay at the fanciest hotels. It's about the experience and the memories for him.

3. Lastly, he would probably also enter a hot dog, Cheezies, or any sugary treat–eating contest. He doesn't deny his affection for confection. It's possible I wouldn't have to even dare him. (Actually, he might just do that anyway, like, for lunch.)

NEAR-DEATH EXPERIENCES
Drew

During a party in London in my early 20s, I walked out onto a 5-foot-deep window ledge on the tenth floor of a building. It was slightly wet and mossy. Nevertheless, I proceeded to step across the corner to another ledge that was a foot lower as everybody remaining on the bigger ledge went back inside. After determining that slick surfaces and stiff drinks don't mix, I attempted to get back inside, but the window on my tiny ledge didn't open. As I made my way back up to the higher ledge, I lost my footing, and in what seemed like slow motion I desperately grabbed at anything I could. It was a sheer drop 100 feet down to the sidewalk. I managed to get my hand wedged into a missing brick and crawled back inside. That was too close for comfort.

I also had a scary road-rage incident. This guy aggressively cut in front of me in traffic and blocked an intersection. He was clearly in the wrong and then proceeded to flip me off out his driver window. So I gave him a sarcastic thumbs-up out my window, at which point he stepped out of his vehicle and came at me yelling, "I'll beat you with a bat!" In an overly calm manner, I got out of my car and responded, "I don't see a bat. Where's your bat?" We went back and forth like this for a minute, and cars started honking as we held up traffic. Then, as though a switch flipped, he pulled out a knife and started screaming that he doesn't need a bat. The only thing between him and me was the door of my car. After a couple swipes I got back in my car and called the police. The guy took off, and who knows if he was ever caught. Sigh.

Jonathan

Early on in my renovation days, before I had taken any construction-site safety training, I'd take on the occasional task knowing there was inherent risk involved. One such time was when I was changing out the breakers on an old, rusted electrical panel. I could not get the screw to turn and foresaw the danger of pushing too hard into the panel. As an idiotic safety precaution, I had JD stand next to me with a 2x4 in case I got electrocuted and couldn't let go of the tool. He would knock me free and remain unharmed, since wood doesn't conduct. As I tried rotating the metal screwdriver again, it kept slipping, so I kept pushing harder and harder to get a grip. All of a sudden, the screwdriver slipped right into the heart of the panel and zapped me like you wouldn't believe. JD didn't have to hit me because I went flying back on my own. I was a little dazed and definitely confused. But at least I still had all my fingers and a heartbeat.

There was one other time that stands out. When I was about 16, I remember I was driving with a buddy, and we were chatting about who knows what, and I remember having the sudden urge to prove my street cred by drag racing solo off an imaginary line and showing him how fast my '82 Oldsmobile Omega could go. Which was something like 0–60 in 2 or 3 minutes. Regardless, I had picked up enough speed that I didn't have time to slow down when I noticed the stop sign I was passing. I wasn't wearing my seatbelt, and I T-boned a pickup truck at full speed. My car was destroyed, and the truck was sent flying a hundred yards in the opposite direction. I had hit my mouth on the steering wheel, splitting my gums wide open, and there was blood everywhere. One moment spent trying to prove something and the only thing I proved was that I wasn't thinking. Fortunately, nobody was seriously injured, but it was a wakeup call.

SUPPORTING THE ARTS

Early on in high school, Drew got a callback to audition for a role as a nerdy science kid in a television series. He found a pair of Coke-bottle glasses to wear for his meeting with the director and producer. The casting people made a big deal out of how cool the specs were and asked where on earth he had found such a prop. Drew thought he had the role in the bag, but he never heard back from them again. Curious to find out who got the part and what they had that he didn't, Drew turned on the show, only to see one of the lead characters now wearing the exact same Coke-bottle glasses as the ones he had been sporting. You'd think they would have at least sent a thank-you card. Or hired him for wardrobe.

WELL, WE DIDN'T SEE THAT COMING
Jonathan

Living as part of a family like ours, inevitably there will be some quick comebacks, smart remarks, and retorts you didn't anticipate. Mom actually kept a journal of all such humorous moments. One was when

JONATHAN: To truly have vision, you must take risks. You must see the world in a way it hasn't been seen.

DREW: Nothing inspires me more than seeing my friends and family succeed. To be genuinely happy for someone close to you is pure joy.

we were around 4 years old. We were out in the middle of nowhere, camping and soaking up all that Mother Nature had to offer. We were nearing the end of our trip, which had just breezed by, when Dad and I went for a stroll down to the lake to see what the fishing scene was like. It could have been the fresh air or the vast mountain ranges that were inspiring me (or, more likely, my underdeveloped grasp of the English language). But I threw my hands on my hips in a mini-superhero pose and sighed, "Wow, Dad. Time is passing like wind."

Another time, only about a year later, we were at the bank with Dad. (Actually, we were pretty much wherever he was, which is why we were nicknamed his shadows.) Standing about 10 feet in front of us was an African-American family with a 2-year-old bouncing around carefree. Dad smiled lovingly. "I remember when you guys were that age." There was a pause, and 5-year-old Drew piped up with innocent wonder: "Were we black, too?"

In more recent years, when a reporter interviewing us at home asked what age we were when we got separate rooms, we couldn't remember for sure. Jonathan turned and asked Mom, who was in town visiting, "Hey, Mom, how old were we when we stopped sleeping in our bunk beds?"

"Twenty-one or twenty-two," she sweetly deadpanned.

WEIRDEST THING PURCHASED RECENTLY
Drew

Lovable weirdo that he is, Jonathan likes to create strange, unique gifts for Jacinta, so he bought an old-school looking Jack-in-the-box that he saw in Montreal. Once he got it back to Vegas, he yanked off the head and replaced it with his own from one of our bobblehead dolls.

Now when the Jon-in-the-box pops up, it's holding a sign that says "I ♥ Jacinta."

Jonathan

A "man garter." I could probably leave it there and you'd be wondering what the heck I'm talking about. Let me explain. You know what a garter is, right? Basically an elastic band that goes around the upper thigh, typically found on a bride or a burlesque dancer. Yep, like that. Drew bought himself one. Except his has been adapted with bands that clip onto his shirt to prevent it from becoming untucked, which I didn't realize was a major issue. Believe me, the first time you walk in on your brother wearing his man-garter, you won't know whether to laugh or cry.

EARLIEST AMBITION

In kindergarten, everyone sat in a circle and announced what they wanted to be when they grew up. There was a long litany of fireman, doctor, policeman, teacher, astronaut, ballerina, etc. Come Jonathan's turn, he stood up in front of the whole class, looked around, and proudly proclaimed, "I'm going to be a flower man." Nobody really knew whether he planned on growing flowers, arranging them, delivering them, or morphing into one, but at that age, everything was exciting and the class applauded.

Drew went through a phase when all he could think about was collecting stamps. You may think he'd scour the planet looking for the rarest finds, but without a driver's license, trust fund, or even an elementary school diploma at this point, he would cut them off of any mail that he came across. This was an interesting way to see postal practices from around the globe, but his lust for stamp-licking was out of control, and he started cutting them off letters Mom and Dad hadn't mailed yet, or he would take their entire roll of unused stamps and put them in his book. Fortunately he grew out of the phase as our parents were about to pack him up and send him to a faraway place . . . assuming they could find the necessary postage.

GHOSTBUSTERS

We both believe in ghosts and love to visit haunted destinations whenever we have the opportunity. The obsession started when traveling in Scotland as little kids, touring all the castles, cathedrals, and ruins we could find. We've been to dozens and dozens of publicly advertised paranormal places without seeing a single spook, but when we were younger and not expecting anything—that's when we got our proof.

Drew is certain he has seen ghosts twice. The first time was with me when we were 6 and exploring in the forest behind our summer camp lodge. It was dusk, and the forest had turned from a fun place to frolic into an eerie environment that sent chills up our spines. At the crest of the hill, we saw a subtle glow coming through the fog. Strange, as there was no road up there. Then, all of a sudden, a strange dog-like beast dove through the trees and came right for us. It chased us down the hill toward the lodge. We were freaking out, and it was gaining on us. We kept glancing over our shoulders to prepare for who it would grab first. Then, without warning, it jumped into the air and vanished like mist.

Then, around the age of 10, after the family checked into an old Scottish castle on vacation, Drew bolted awake in the middle of the night when he heard a sound. He saw an old woman peering into our bedroom window. Drew froze, unsure of what to do and utterly petrified. She just stared intensely for about 30 seconds, then slipped away into the darkness. Drew immediately burrowed under the protection of his covers and stayed there for the rest of the night. The next morning at breakfast, Drew brought up the peeping hag and how creepy she was. Dad laughed and told Drew that no one could possibly be spying on him. Drew was certain he had seen the woman. Dad told him to go look out the window. When he did, Drew saw that the castle was high on a cliff—there was nothing but a sheer drop outside the window.

SPEAKING OF SCOTLAND

Everybody knows we love sushi. Believe it or not, being Scottish, we didn't grow up savoring raw fish. What was the family favorite (except for JD, who is the pickiest eater alive) for us? Haggis! Scotland's national dish—a large, boiled sausage encased in a sheep's stomach, containing minced sheep's heart, liver, and lungs, mixed with oatmeal, onion, and suet, and seasoned with nutmeg and mace. (In the U.S., sheep's lungs are banned, so they use tongue instead).

It's amazing. Trust us! Haggis out of a can is delicious, too. If you like real German sausage, you'll like haggis. Basically the same ingredients. And it's not really wrapped in a sheep's stomach . . . anymore. Seriously, don't knock it until you've tried it on a bun. By the way, it's best served to a bagpipe tune.

SEAMS LIKE OLD TIMES
Jonathan

Drew pretty much rips a pair of pants every week. Usually doing a whole lotta nothing. Most of the time, it's the butt that tears, and

I'm going to go out on a limb and guess it's because he over-tailors everything he owns. He has ripped pants doing a cartwheel, walking, standing still, sliding down a rail, and riding a mechanical bull, which exposed purple underwear to the appreciative crowd of onlookers.

One time when I was removing an old window, Drew bet $20 that he could do a ninja dive through it with flawless somersault form and land perfectly on the deck. He miraculously pulled it off without touching the sides at all. Somewhat in disbelief, I simply stepped through the opening to give him his cash, caught the crotch of my jeans on a nail, and ripped my pants completely open—with cameras rolling. I felt less than athletic and a little breezy downstairs.

Drew

Long before *Property Brothers*, Jonathan was actually the suit guy. I lived mostly in sweats or jeans. It was a complete role reversal because Jonathan owned three or four suits, and I'd borrow them whenever I needed to. For our birthday one year, I made Jonathan a suit out of one-dollar bills that he had to painstakingly separate to purchase a nice outfit. I'm not sure what it was that clicked in me, but all of a sudden I liked having my own tailored attire. It started with one nice jacket, then a suit, then another—to the point where now I could open a men's clothing store with my wardrobe, and Jonathan is definitely my most active customer.

Jonathan doesn't buy expensive clothes for fear he'll just lose them like the trail of jackets, vests, sweaters, and hats he's left behind at ball games, concerts, construction sites, and rental homes on location. Costliest casualty of our early twenties? The $700 titanium e-wire Oakley sunglasses he left on top of a Metro ticket machine and remembered ten stops later. Not surprisingly, when he went back, they were gone. This is why he doesn't trust himself with nice things.

WHAT WE'RE PACKING

We're pretty much always traveling. We'll move into temporary quarters on location for 3 to 6 months, and when we're not shooting, we're on a plane to do appearances, commercials, meetings, or events somewhere else. Here's the dish on how we roll:

Drew

Jonathan travels light. He brings his two dogs, plus dog crates, food, and toys. For himself, he'll pack a hat, a variety of shirts—a good chunk of them plaid—six pairs of jeans (two x heavy fade, two x medium fade, two x light fade), two pairs of boots, and a piano keyboard. He takes lessons, but I think he mainly uses it as a drying rack.

Jonathan

Drew ships several pallets of belongings. He and Linda have so much stuff, they actually need extra bedrooms on the road to use as closets, and it takes them weeks to pack when changing cities. I can have all of my stuff packed in less than a day. Drew brings dozens of suits, hundreds of ties and socks, and a crazy number of shoes. He usually ships clothing racks as well. He always brings a custom box with about twenty watches that match every outfit under the sun. And his protein powder, of course. I won't go through Customs with him. He packs it in neat little baggies he puts in his suitcase. I think the U.S. Customs officers who detained him on the way back from a Mexican vacation still think there's something shady going on there.

HAIR TRAGEDY

WHAT WE ALWAYS FORGET
Jonathan

It's a known fact on a construction site that tape measures, pencils, and hammers are commodities that frequently vanish into the abyss. Nobody can explain where they go, but I'm assuming it's the same place as missing socks in the dryer. We have the same problem on the road—but with larger, stranger items. We predominantly work from home, so we frequently use a color laser printer. They always get left behind or go missing when we leave one location and head to another. We've probably lost a dozen over the years. Either somebody is hoarding them or there's a lot of people enjoying color printing at our expense.

Also, when traveling with the pups, I like the living situation to be as comfortable and similar to home as possible. So anytime I have a terrace, I'll install this clever dog gate into the sliding glass door. It's a tall 12-inch-wide panel that attaches to the slider and has the perfect little dog door at the bottom. It means the dogs can go in and out as they please, the place is secure, and the bugs are staying out. These "add-on access" solutions are pretty substantial and cost upwards of $500. And every time I change cities, they disappear. I feel like Gracie and Stewie are cashing in on the dog-door black market with them.

NAME GAME
Jonathan

Our parents say it's only a coincidence that everyone's name in our family starts with a "J" except for Drew, who was named Andrew after the patron saint of Scotland. Matthew, Sean, and Seamus were close contenders as boy names, and for a while, so were Ricky, Peter, Clint and . . . Scott. If we'd been girls, we would've been Robyn, Emma, Mary, or Morag, which is a Scottish variation of Sarah. Maude and Charlotte fell off in the semifinals.

As Drew was a complete surprise when they delivered him, Dad rushed downstairs and bought Mom two dozen roses and grabbed two bottles of Scotch each for the four hospital staff in the delivery room. They had to scramble to decide which of the back-up baby names they'd give to the unexpected bundle of joy. There's a part of me that wishes it was Morag Scott Scott.

THE NEXT GENERATION

I hope my future children inherit . . .

Drew: My drive and focus.

Jonathan: My humor, my patience, my passion, and my dedication to people.

But don't end up with . . .

Drew: MY LOUD TALKING.

Jonathan: My hyperactivity and short attention span.

WHAT WE'RE FORBIDDEN TO DO BY CONTRACT
Drew

We've been asked on many occasions if we wear our hair or dress the way we do because of the shows. Not particularly. We don't actually have a lot of contractual restrictions, but we try to stay mindful as a courtesy and in an attempt to be a good partner.

Contractually, we're not supposed to do anything extreme with our physical appearance like get butt implants, dye our hair pink, or get a nose ring. Other than that, our contracts are more focused on our safety. We're not allowed to do anything that puts us at heightened risk like skydiving, bull riding, bungee jumping, or motocross racing. I guess they don't want the show to become *Property Brother*. Oh, and also important to note, we can't do any nudity in film or commit any crimes. Well, that's boring. Haha.

HOW WE ALMOST DIDN'T FIND OUT
WE WERE GETTING A SHOW
Drew

After years of trying to break into the business, my intense networking efforts had sparked interest from a major Canadian production company, but after we filmed a sizzle reel, there was nothing but crickets for months. Meanwhile, Scott Real Estate was growing like gangbusters. To thank our clients, we would give away movie tickets, which we bought in bulk from the Cineplex theater chain. I had been waiting on a severely delayed big order when a call came in from a woman who barely got the words "Hi, I'm calling from Cine—" out of her mouth before I cut her off and started expressing my frustration over what was taking so long. I said it was unacceptable and that we might take our business elsewhere.

"Excuse me?" said the woman on the other end.

"Our tickets, when are you sending the tickets?" I repeated.

"I don't think I was clear," the woman apologized. "This is Sarah from Cineflix Productions. We want to give you a pilot."

Whoops. That was close.

MAY THE FORCE BE WITH US
Jonathan

Drew and William Shatner engaged in a hilarious "frenemies" war on Twitter after we met Bill a couple of years ago, and he began following us. He would tweet along with the show and share his thoughts. When he noted that I was his favorite and Drew wasn't his cup of tea, Drew hopped on and responded with a clever dig. It was on! Bill called him #TooTightTeeDrew, and Drew would rebut by posting old pictures of Captain Kirk wearing clothes that were over-tailored. The feud ended when Drew sent Bill a Scott Brothers gift basket with a "Team Drew" shirt for international friendship day and gave a shout-out to a charity Bill supported. The truce lasted for about a month. To this day, you can still catch them poking fun at each other on Twitter.

WHO MAY I SAY IS CALLING?
Jonathan

Sometimes we can't tell ourselves apart. We used to share a pager (yes, I said it) and a cell phone for work, and we would leave voice messages for each other saying things like, "Hey, give me a call when you get a sec." This led to frequent confusion when we'd forget who left the message with everything going on and wonder whose voice it was. Especially bad if we were playing phone tag with a subcontractor or supplier. "Bill wants you to call" could end up with Bill getting two calls, or none because we also knew several Bills, or assumed the message was for the other brother and he had responded. Our communication needed work. We even contemplated using phony accents so that we'd know who was talking. Seriously. Even when calling home to Mom and Dad, they said it was almost impossible to tell us apart on the phone. But in one of my proudest moments, Mom told Drew her secret for telling us apart: "Jonathan uses bigger words." Haha.

CARBON COPY BENEFITS
Drew

We do our own voiceover narrations for the shows, but in an emergency, as we sound VERY similar, we can play the other. There have been three or four such situations to date when we were up against a deadline, and production had forgotten to get a line from the one or the other. Jonathan calls his Drew voice "The Anal Realtor," and articulates his words more precisely and makes his voice a little more nasally. I call my Jonathan voice "The Dumb Contractor" and make my tone slightly more bass and less precise. Ever notice Jonathan slurs a little?

Confusing people was a favorite vacation pastime, and it's so easy for twins. There was a hotel we were staying in where all the guest floors looked exactly the same coming off the extremely slow elevator. We had discovered that if one of us hung out in that area nonchalantly, the people in the elevator would see us and not think anything of it. The other one of us would have pressed the button on the next floor and would be waiting in the exact same position, exact same clothes, when the doors opened. We'd just keep racing up the stairs to do it on floor after floor. The people inside were SO confused and would think the elevator was going nowhere. After three or four floors of this, they'd eventually clue in and either laugh or yell at us.

Other than these situations, the usual conveniences are no more than logistical pleasantries. For example, we each carry an additional

ID for the other in case we ever have to do a pickup or sign for something not addressed to us. Shh, don't tell anybody . . . but it has proven to be one of the most valuable time-saving advantages that only twins can enjoy.

THE Z FACTOR
Drew

I'm pretty sure this little tidbit isn't something Jonathan ever told somebody on a first date, but he sometimes sleeps with his eyes open. That's right, it's frighteningly creepy. They're wide open, like they're waiting for the mortician to put quarters over them. Add to that: He occasionally sleepwalks. Aaand you have all the makings of a horror film.

DOGS' BEST FRIEND
Jonathan

When anybody thinks of a rugged, manly contractor (such as yours truly! Come on, work with me), they'd probably assume he'd pair best with a Labrador, Rottweiler, German Shepherd, or some other oversized K-9 wearing a cool neckerchief. That's old-school thinking . . . it's the 21st century, and we no longer judge a man by the size of his beast.

I've always been a dog guy. I love their loyalty, unwavering affection, and the random weirdness they endlessly entertain me with. But I'm also a realist. I have a crazy schedule filled with lots of travel, and a big dog would be nearly impossible. I remember it was very difficult to transport JD's 150-pound Rotty, and his cage wouldn't even fit in the cargo hold of most planes. Not only can my fur kids fit under the seats in front of Drew and me, but I also have endless friends who offer to babysit/steal them. They really are very self-reliant, and as easy-going as it goes with new people. And a side benefit: Their poop is a tenth the size of a German Shepherd's. Makes for VERY easy cleanup.

Stewie and Gracie have successfully worked themselves into the fabric of our family. Mom and Dad love them to pieces, and Jacinta's parents have made more requests to visit the puppies than even us. Linda is totally allergic to Gracie, but deals with the sniffles because she likes the cuddles. Drew likes being the cool uncle and will randomly come over when I'm not home to dress them up and take puppy selfies. The funniest thing in the world is that when JD comes over, Gracie loses her mind. She is obsessed with him and screams like a banshee because she's so excited.

ASSAULT BY CUTE BUT OVER-ENTHUSIASTIC CHILDREN

Drew

Maybe it's that we're big kids at heart, or that we never matured fully into adulthood, but we seem to get along exceptionally well with little ones. I'd lose count if I tried to remember all the funny moments we've had with kids on our shows.

Jonathan was chased down and flattened by two little girls in a pink Barbie Jeep. They didn't even hesitate when they drove over him not once, but twice. Jonathan wasn't hurt, and the Barbie Jeep treadmarks came out in the wash.

Jonathan also took one for the team when he was filming a reno check-in on *Property Brothers*, and the homeowners' little boy started getting excited to the point of bouncing off the walls of his new home. To burn off a little of the energy, Jonathan suggested a little on-the-spot boogie-ing. The boy apparently only knew one dance move called the Punch Your Contractor Square in the Crotch. Jonathan collapsed to the ground, and his voice has never fully recovered.

I've also had some unexpected and hilarious moments with the juniors of the species. We were shooting *Brother vs. Brother*, and our first assistant director brought her daughter to the set. She's this absolute angel with a smile that would melt even the toughest of hearts. Apparently, she had cast out all her dolls and toys and was only interested in one thing—the Drew bobblehead. Seriously, she was gripping onto plastic me like a post-apocalyptic squirrel that had found the planet's last nut. She squeezed it so tight the arm broke, and she STILL wouldn't let it go. I mean, I can't blame her . . . I'm very huggable. But I'm pretty sure it made Jonathan jealous.

I have fallen victim to countless unsolicited toddler makeovers that left me ready for a drag show, as well as numerous spontaneous dance parties hosted by bossy prima ballerinas who insist I twirl and giggle. But I don't complain.

I consider all of this a warmup to when I can play dress-up and dance with my own kids. I've never pictured myself being a father until I met Linda and when I finally am . . . I certainly don't plan on growing up any further.

For information about permission to reproduce
selections from this book, write to trade.
permissions@hmhco.com or to Permissions,
Houghton Mifflin Harcourt Publishing Company,
3 Park Avenue, 19th Floor, New York, New York
10016.

hmhco.com

Library of Congress Cataloging-in-Publication
Data is available.

ISBN 978-1-328-77147-6 (hbk)

ISBN 978-1-328-77098-1 (ebk)

ISBN 978-1-328-94163-3 (hbk)

ISBN 978-1-328-96747-3 (hbk)

Book design by Rita Sowins
Composition by Eugenie S. Delaney

Printed in the United States of America
DOC 10 9 8 7 6 5 4 3 2 1